Presented to:

_____

By:

_____

Date:

_____

Honor Books® is an imprint of
Cook Communications Ministries, Colorado Springs, CO 80918
Cook Communications, Paris, Ontario
Kingsway Communications Ltd., Eastbourne, England

*Water from the Rock: Meditations on Peace and Purpose—
Timeless Writings to Strengthen Your Faith and Anchor Your Soul*
© 2005 by BORDON BOOKS

All rights reserved under International Copyright Law. Contents and/or cover may not be reproduced in whole or in part in any form without the express written consent of the Publisher. For information, write Cook Communications Ministries, 4050 Lee Vance View, Colorado Springs, CO 80918.

First Printing, 2005
Printed in the United States of America
2 3 4 5 6 Printing / Year 09 08 07 06 05

Developed by Bordon Books
Manuscript written by Christi Flagg
Designed by Koechel, Peterson and Associates

Scripture quotations marked NIV are taken from the *Holy Bible, New International Version.*® NIV®. Copyright © 1973, 1978, 1984 by International Bible Society. Used by permission of Zondervan Publishing House. All rights reserved; KJV are taken from the *King James Version* of the Bible; MSG are taken from *The Message*, copyright © by Eugene H. Peterson, 1993, 1994, 1995, 1996. Used by permission of NavPress Publishing Group; NASB are taken from the *New American Standard Bible*. Copyright © The Lockman Foundation 1960, 1962, 1963, 1968, 1971, 1972, 1973, 1975, 1977, 1995. Used by permission; ASV are taken from the *American Standard Version*. Copyright © 1901 by Thomas Nelson & Sons and copyright © 1929 by International Council of Religious Education; NKJV are taken from *The New King James Version*. Copyright © 1979, 1980, 1982 by Thomas Nelson, Inc; NLT are taken from the *Holy Bible, New Living Translation*, copyright © 1996. Used by permission of Tyndale House Publishers, Inc., Wheaton, Illinois 60189. All rights reserved; NCV are taken from *The Holy Bible, New Century Version*, copyright © 1987, 1988, 1991 by Word Publishing, Dallas, Texas 75039. Used by permission; CEV are taken from the *Contemporary English Version*, copyright © 1991, 1992, 1995 by the American Bible Society. Used by permission.

Antiquated spellings, vocabulary, and punctuation usage in the selected texts of some of the historical writers quoted in this book have been edited to conform to present-day American English usage so that the edited quotations will convey the same meaning to the contemporary reader that the original writers intended to express.

ISBN: 1-56292-365-X

WATER FROM THE ROCK

MEDITATIONS ON PEACE AND PURPOSE:

CLASSIC WRITINGS TO STRENGTHEN YOUR FAITH AND ANCHOR YOUR SOUL

Inspiration and Motivation for the Seasons of Life

COOK COMMUNICATIONS MINISTRIES
Colorado Springs, CO • Paris, Ontario
KINGSWAY COMMUNICATIONS LTD
Eastbourne, England

Table of Contents

Introduction 9
God's Purpose for Us 10
The Water from the Rock Brings Peace 12
Peace in His Presence 14
The Heart of God's Purpose Is Love 16
The Purpose of Saint Patrick's Prayer 18
Peace from Anxiety 20
The Purpose of Simplicity 22
The Purpose of the Holy Spirit Is Freedom from Sin 24
Only Christ Will Do 26
Peace Beyond Understanding 28
The Peace of Knowing Christ 30
The Purpose of Life—to Love God 32
Peace and Surrender 34
The Purpose of Brokenness 36
Peace in the Assurance of Salvation 38
Peace in God's Presence 40
God's Purpose for Trials 41
The Purpose of Holiness 43
Peace in Submission 44
Purpose in Prayer 46
Peace of Mind 48
The Purpose of Silent Prayer 49
Silent Prayer—Focusing on God Alone 51
Preserving Peace in Love 52
Purpose to Know Yourself 53
How to Seek and Maintain Peace 55
God's Will 57
The Purpose of Guilt 59
The Peace of Christ 62
Jesus' Purpose 64
The Purpose of Pruning 66
God Is a God of Peace 67
The Purpose of Purity 68
Look Up for Peace 70

Pray for Peace	72
The Peace of God's Firm Foundation	74
The Purpose of Dry Times	76
Peace and a Good Conscience	78
Purpose to Pray	80
God's Purposes Cannot Be Frustrated	82
God's Amazing Purpose	84
Peace with Humility	87
God's Purpose in Everything	89
The Purpose of Suffering Is Patience	91
The Purpose in God's Truth	93
Peace with a Pure Heart	95
Peace Comes from a Love Focused on God	97
Peace from Impurity	99
Peace with God's Limitless Love	101
The Way to a Pure Heart	103
The Purpose of Prayer Is Purity	105
Longing for Peace	107
The Purpose of Living	109
The Purpose of Love	111
God's Purposes Are for Our Good	113
God's Ways with Backsliders	115
Determining God's Purpose in the Little and Big Things	117
Peace and Blessings in Suffering	120
The Peace of Healing	123
The Purpose of Servant Leaders	124
A Fixed Purpose to Know God	126
The Purpose of Shepherding	128
Our Purpose Is to Worship God	130
The Purpose of Life	132
The Purpose of the Holy Spirit Is Power	134
The Purpose of Continuing Prayer	136
The Purpose of Dreams	138
The Peace of Unity in Prayer	140
The Purpose of Moses	142
An Instrument of Peace	144
Peace with God's Forgiveness	146
The Triumph of God's Good Purpose	148

Trust and Peace	151
The Purpose of the Bible	152
Peace in God's Love	154
The Purpose and Blessing of Thanksgiving	156
The Purpose of God's Love	158
The Peace of Abiding in Christ in Prayer	160
The Purpose of Christ-like Forgiveness	162
A Reason for Our Peace	164
The Purpose of the Church—To Be Led by Christ	166
The Purpose of Revival	168
Peace of Conscience	170
The Purpose of the Body	172
The Purpose and Necessity of Emotions	174
The Purpose of Surrendering to Christ	176
The Purpose of Spiritual Discipline	178
The Path of Peace	180
The Purpose of Joshua's Leadership	181
The Purpose of Church	183
The Purpose of Meditating on Scripture for Prayer	184
The Peace of Friendship	186
The Purpose of the Trinity	188
God's Purposes for Us Aren't Always Logical	190
The Purpose of Spiritual Power Is Holiness	192
Assurance and Peace	194
The Purpose of Christ's Judgment for Christians	196
Peace with Doubts	198
The Purposes of God's Promises	200
The Purpose of Abiding in Prayer	201
God's Eternal Purpose	203
The Wisdom of Peace	204
The Purpose of the Holy Spirit Is to Teach	206
A Purpose for the Lost	208
Inner Peace	210
Comfort in God Alone	212
A Purpose for Depression	214
Peace for the Doubting Christian	216
God's Purpose for His People—Preach the Good News	218
Go in Peace	220

Introduction

Water from the Rock: Classic Writings on Peace and Purpose is a devotional filled with the writings of great men and women of God—writings that we believe will open your heart to God's peace and your mind to a better understanding of His purpose for your life.

We pray that your faith will be strengthened and your heart encouraged as you read excerpts from the teachings of great Christians such as Dwight L. Moody, Charles H. Spurgeon, Hannah Whitall Smith, Annie Johnson Flint, John Wesley, John Bunyan, Evelyn Underhill and many more. These timeless insights of well-known and not so well-known classic Christian writers are sure to leave you better equipped to live in harmony with your Creator. And like water from a rock in the midst of the desert, we hope they will refresh your thirsty soul.

[God] split the rocks in the desert and gave them water as abundant as the seas; he brought streams out of a rocky crag and made water flow down like rivers.

PSALM 78:15-16 NIV

God's Purpose for Us

Whether you turn to the right or to the left, your ears will hear a voice behind you, saying, "This is the way; walk in it."
ISAIAH 30:21 NIV

God has promised to guide and teach us, but it may be hard for us to distinguish His will from our own. The first thing to do is to align our choices with Scripture. Then listen to the advice of wise friends. And finally, or perhaps, continually, pray and see if God has a definite direction He would have us take. John A. Broadus (1878-1958), a Southern Baptist minister and chaplain in the Civil War, offers these insights:

"How do we ascertain God's will? Partly from our own consciences aided by the general conscience of mankind, but this is by no means an infallible test. To some extent, we may seek the best judgment and advice of others. It is always important to have the mind stored with Scripture. Then we can pray and trust we are doing God's will."
-JOHN A. BROADUS

There are times when we pray but we feel no obvious answer—there are other times when He does give a slight push toward the right or the left. And then there are times when we haven't prayed yet, and God will speak in a booming voice and point the way.

Many of us find ourselves irritated because God doesn't speak in an obvious way.

"I didn't understand why as usual God couldn't give me a loud or obvious answer? ... Why does God always use dreams, intuition, memory, phone calls, vague stirrings in my heart? I would say that this really doesn't work for me at all. Except that it does."

-ANNE LAMOTT

God often speaks in obvious ways—and then again there are times when He does not. Don't become discouraged if you find yourself face-to-face with the silence of God. Many great Christians have had the same experience. It is in these times that your faith will be tested and proven. Trust in God, cling to Him, recognizing that He will always act in your best interest. He loves you.

"If we make a quietness within ourselves, if we silence all desires and opinions, and if with love ... we bind our whole soul to think, 'Thy will be done,' the thing which, after that, we feel sure we should do ... is the will of God."

-SIMONE WEIL

The Water from the Rock Brings Peace

"The Lamb at the center of the throne will be their shepherd;
he will lead them to springs of living water.
And God will wipe away every tear from their eyes."
REVELATION 7:17 NIV

When Moses struck a rock in the desert and water poured out for the thirsty Israelites, it was a clear example of how a loving God will miraculously and abundantly provide for His people. But God doesn't just provide for our physical needs, He cares about our emotional and spiritual needs as well.

Jesus told the Samaritan woman at the well that He could give her living water, water that would satisfy. He meant himself. Later Jesus said, "If anyone is thirsty, let him come to me and drink. Whoever believes in me, as the Scripture has said, streams of living water will flow from within him" (John 7:37-38 NIV). In the next verse, John explains that "by this he meant the Spirit, whom those who believed in him were later to receive." Jesus, or God, in the form of the Holy Spirit, is the water from the rock that dwells within us and flows from our lives.

When we ask Christ to be our Lord and invite His Spirit to enter our lives with God's power, we are transformed. God's Spirit flows through us, and the passage Jesus quotes from Isaiah is fulfilled.

This passage in Isaiah 32 says that each of us in the kingdom of righteousness will be "like a shelter from the wind and a refuge from the storm, like streams of water in the desert and the shadow of a great rock in a thirsty land" (Isaiah 32:2 NIV). When the kingdom of God lives in us, not only will we receive living water in a dry world, but also we will be that living water for others around us.

The Water from the Rock, that is, God, brings us every blessing for our own lives and for those we come in contact with. He brings us peace and purpose for every day. Christ said, "If you knew . . . who it is that asks you for a drink, you would have asked him and he would have given you living water" (John 4:10 NIV). The following collection of excerpts from classic Christian writers will give a better understanding and awareness of who Christ is and how to ask for more of His Spirit.

Peace in His Presence

"God's kingdom is like a treasure hidden in a field for years and then accidentally found by a trespasser. The finder is ecstatic—what a find!—and proceeds to sell everything he owns to raise money and buy that field. Or, God's kingdom is like a jewel merchant on the hunt for excellent pearls. Finding one that is flawless, he immediately sells everything and buys it."

MATTHEW 13:44-46 MSG

The secret fear of many Christians is that God is a jerk, that He doesn't like them, and that if they gave Him any more of their life, He'd make them miserable and unhappy. So we wander around on tiptoes trying to be just good enough on our own that we won't need God's help or leading. We pray and worship God only at church and keep Him out of the rest of our lives because we fear what He would do there.

But God is not a power-hungry jerk who sits around thinking how He can strip the fun and enjoyment out of our lives. God has all the power already. He created us and continues to keep us running. At any moment, He could take control of or stop our lives, but He doesn't. God loves us. God wants us to love Him in return and to enjoy our lives freely in His presence.

When He wants us to freely give Him control of our lives, it is because He wants to give us greater joy. And He is that greater joy. God's presence is sufficient to make everything else on earth worthless. When King Solomon wrote at the beginning of Ecclesiastes, "Meaningless! Meaningless! Utterly meaningless! Everything is meaningless," he had everything. He had riches, power, God-given wisdom, hundreds of wives, armies, friends, everything. And yet He saw that everything in this world is worthless and empty without God.

Instead of fearing God and running from intimacy with Him, spend time in His presence. Delight in His company. God loves you; you are His child. He will give you peace and joy.

The Heart of God's Purpose is Love

A day in Thy courts is better than a thousand outside.
I would rather stand at the threshold of the house of my God,
than dwell in the tents of wickedness.
PSALM 84:10 NASB

The best thing that we could ever imagine is experiencing God and being in His presence. He is good. Our lives are worth all the troubles and pain, if the result is that we are resting in the presence of God. In the following excerpt, Richard Baxter (1615-1691) writes of the culmination of our desires, the Christian life with Christ, as His friend, servant, body, bride, co-heir, and love.

Be of good cheer, the time is at hand when God will be near—as near as you desire. You shall dwell in His family. Is that enough? It is better to be a doorkeeper in the house of God, than to dwell in the tents of wickedness. You shall stand before Him, about His throne, in the room with Him, in His presence.

Would you still desire to be nearer? You shall be His child, and He your Father. You shall be an heir of His kingdom, and even the spouse of His Son.

And what more could you desire? You shall be a member of the body of His Son; He shall be your head. You shall be one with Him, who is one with the Father. For He Himself has desired, "That they all may be one; even as You, Father, are in Me and I in You that they also may be one in Us, so that the world may believe that You sent Me. The glory which You have given Me I have given to them, that they may be one, just as We are one: I in them, and You in Me, that they may be perfected in unity, so that the world may know that You sent Me, and loved them, even as You have loved Me" (John 17:21-23 NASB).

-RICHARD BAXTER

What an amazing chance we have to be beloved by God and included in His plans. As Christians, we aren't just doorkeepers in the house of the Lord. We are His children.

The Purpose of Saint Patrick's Prayer

You are my hiding place; you will protect me from trouble and surround me with songs of deliverance.
PSALM 32:7 NIV

Many people have heard of Saint Patrick and know that his symbol is a clover or shamrock. However, few people know what made Saint Patrick both a saint and a hero. Saint Patrick brought Christianity to the attention of Ireland. And through him, Christians were free to worship without fear of persecution.

During the pagan festival of spring, Saint Patrick and his followers celebrated Easter by lighting a small fire. This was a rebellious act, because no other fires were to be burning except the giant one in the Druid celebration.

He and his followers were promptly arrested and put on trial before the Druids and before the king of Ireland. He prayed the entire way to the prison and before the trial. When Saint Patrick appeared before the king, they were acquitted when he spoke up and convinced the king of the truth of Christianity. Legend says he used a clover to explain the Trinity to the king. He took a bold step, and instead of being martyred, Saint Patrick became a hero.

Saint Patrick's prayer asks for wisdom, protection, guidance, and power from God. It is one we can read aloud for strength and encouragement.

*I bind me to-day,
God's might to direct me,
God's power to protect me,
God's wisdom for learning,
God's eye for discerning,
God's ear for my hearing,
God's word for my clearing.*

*God's hand for my cover,
God's path to pass over,
God's buckler to guard me,
God's army to ward me,
Against snares of the devil,
Against vice's temptation,
Against wrong inclination,
Against men who plot evil,
Near or afar, with many or few.*

*Christ near,
Christ here,
Christ be with me,
Christ beneath me,*

*Christ within me,
Christ behind me,
Christ be o'er me,
Christ before me.*

*Christ in the left and the right,
Christ hither and thither,
Christ in the sight,
Of each eye that shall seek me,*

*In each ear that shall hear,
In each mouth that shall speak me—
Christ not the less,
In each heart I address.*

*I bind me to-day on the Triune I call,
With faith in the Trinity—Unity—God over all!*

-SAINT PATRICK, TRANSLATED BY DR. GEORGE SIGERSON

Peace from Anxiety

*[Jesus said,] "Peace I leave with you,
My peace I give to you."*
JOHN 14:27 NKJV

In the following passage, Oswald Chambers (1874-1917) points to Jesus as the only source of peace:

Are you anxious just now, distracted by the waves and billows of life? Are you still finding no well of peace or joy or comfort; is all barren? Then look up and receive the undisturbed peace of the Lord Jesus.

Are you looking to Jesus now and handing Him your problems, and are you then receiving from Him peace? If so, He will be a gracious blessing of peace in and through you. But if you try to worry your problems out by yourself, you obliterate His presence in your life.

We get anxious because we have been focusing on the problems; we have not been considering Him. When one goes to Jesus Christ the confusion goes, because in Him there is no confusion. And then, our only concern is to abide in Him.

So, lay it all out before Him, and in the face of difficulty, bereavement, and sorrow, hear Him say, "Let not your heart be troubled."

-OSWALD CHAMBERS

All your anxiety, all your care,
Bring to the mercy seat, leave it there,
Never a burden He cannot bear,
Never a friend like Jesus!

-EDWARD H. JOY

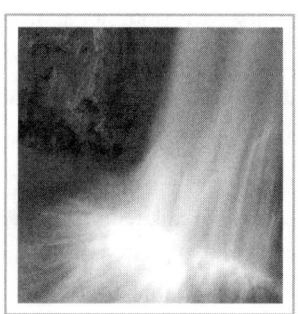

The Purpose of Simplicity

The meek will inherit the land and enjoy great peace.
PSALM 37:11 NIV

It is often hard not to get discouraged when we feel like we aren't intelligent or spiritual enough to understand the Bible or to be "good Christians." Books like *The Bible Code* popularize the hidden messages and secrets in the Word of God. Those of us who don't read Hebrew or Greek tend to feel like we cannot understand God's Word without the interpretation of a genius, a prophet, or someone who's at least been to a seminary.

However, God's message isn't just for a special intellectual or spiritual hierarchy. Instead, God's message is to the humble and the meek. Jesus said, "I praise you, Father, Lord of heaven and earth, because you have hidden these things from the wise and learned, and revealed them to little children," and, "unless you change and become like little children, you will never enter the kingdom of heaven" (Matthew 11:25 and 18:3 NIV). So if there are any hidden messages in the Bible, they won't reveal anything new or vital, but will instead support and affirm God's clear message.

Christ didn't speak in riddles, but to reach the lost sheep. He gave simple illustrations from daily life with examples from farming, fishing, and eating. Modern evangelists like Charles Finney and Dwight L. Moody made sure that they preached and spoke in simple words that children could understand. If children could understand their teachings of God, then their parents would also understand and the gospel would spread.

We need not worry because we aren't genius scholars. Jesus spoke simply to the people. Many of His words were written to fishermen. It definitely helps to read study books and attend Bible studies, but the best way to understand the Bible is to read the Bible. Christ gave us the Holy Spirit, whose job it is to teach us all things and to remind us of everything Christ has said to us. (See John 14:26.) We need not fear not understanding the Bible. Even if we obey what little of the Bible we understand, we will be great in the eyes of God.

So if you are frustrated and feeling dull and unable to understand God's Word, simply pray for understanding and sit down with your Bible. God will bless you and give you understanding.

I will put my law within them—write it on their hearts!—and be their God. And they will be my people. They will no longer go around setting up schools to teach each other about God. They'll know me firsthand, the dull and the bright, the smart and the slow.

JEREMIAH 31:33-34 MSG

The Purpose of the Holy Spirit is Freedom from Sin

May the God of hope fill you with all joy and peace in believing, that you may abound in hope by the power of the Holy Spirit.
ROMANS 15:13 NKJV

Christ was God in the form of man. He was without sin, yet He died for our sins. We were separate from God because we sin. But when we call upon the name of Christ, we are saved; we accept His cleansing forgiveness, and we are holy before God.

But Christ didn't just take care of our past sin; He left us the Holy Spirit, who would teach us all things and give us the power to heal, to cast out demons, and most of all to be like Christ.

Many unbelievers argue that it would be unfair of God to make us with the ability to sin, but still judge us when we do. However, God is a just God, who longs for an open, loving relationship with all people. He also gave us, through the painful death of His Son, the purity necessary to be in His presence and reflect His glory.

We need not worry that God is mean or unfair. He's not a power-hungry tyrant. Instead, He's a loving Father who longs for His children to be safe and at peace in His care. And through the power of the Holy Spirit, we can do just that.

Earnestness is good and impressive: genius is gifted and great. Thought kindles and inspires, but it takes a diviner endowment, and more powerful energy than earnestness or genius or thought to break the chains of sin, to win estranged and deprived hearts to God, to repair the breaches and restore the Church to her old ways of purity and power. Nothing but the anointing of the Holy Spirit can do this.

-E. M. BOUNDS

Only Christ Will Do

I resolved to know nothing . . . except Jesus.
1 CORINTHIANS 2:2 NIV

There is no way that we as humans can work and gain inner peace. Peace does not come from practicing Christian disciplines. The Scottish Presbyterian pastor and writer, Reverend Horatius Bonar (1808-1889) explains that we can find peace only in Christ.

I knew an awakened soul who, in the bitterness of his spirit, set himself to work and pray in order to get peace. He doubled the amount of his devotions, saying to himself, "Surely God will give me peace." But the peace did not come.

He set up family worship times, saying, "Surely God will give me peace." But the peace came not. At last he thought of having a prayer meeting in his house as an answer to his problem. He decided upon the night; called his neighbors; and prepared himself for leading the meeting by writing a prayer and learning it by heart. As he finished learning it, getting ready for the meeting, he threw it down on the table saying, "Surely that will do, God will give me peace now."

In that moment, a still small voice seemed to speak in his ear, saying, "No, that will not do; but Christ will do."

Straightway the scales fell from his eyes, and the burden from his shoulders. Peace poured in like a river. "Christ will do," became the guiding principle for his life.

-REV. HORATIUS BONAR

Peace Beyond Understanding

The peace of God, which transcends all understanding, will guard your hearts and your minds in Christ Jesus.
PHILIPPIANS 4:7 NIV

Without God and His forgiveness, we have no peace. Sin and guilt will plague us, and the fear of both God and the world remains. However, with conversion and repentance of sin, a strong peace dwells in our hearts. The evangelist Charles Finney (1792-1875) experienced this peace that passes understanding alone in the woods outside his town after his conversion.

I found that my mind had become wonderfully quiet and peaceful. I said to myself, "What is this? I must have grieved the Holy Spirit entirely away. I have lost all my conviction. I do not have a particle of concern about my soul, and it must be that the Spirit has left me. Indeed, I never was so far from being concerned about my salvation in my life!"

But how was I to account for the quiet of my mind? I tried to recall my convictions, to get back again the load of sin under which I had been laboring. But all sense of sin, all consciousness of present sin or guilt, had departed from me. I said to myself, "What is this, that I cannot arouse any sense of guilt in my soul, as great a sinner as I am?" I tried in vain to make myself anxious about my present state. I was so quiet and peaceful that I tried to feel concerned about it.

But no matter what view I took of it, I could not be anxious at all about my soul and my spiritual state. The repose of my mind was unspeakably great. I never can describe it in words. The thought of God was sweet to my mind, and the most profound spiritual tranquility had taken full possession of me.

I could now see and understand what was meant by the passage, "Having been justified by faith, we have peace with God through our Lord Jesus Christ" (Romans 5:1 NKJV). I could see that, from the moment I had believed up in the woods, all sense of condemnation had entirely dropped out of my mind, and I could not feel a sense of guilt or condemnation by any effort that I could make. My sins were gone, and my sense of guilt was gone, as if I had never sinned.

-CHARLES FINNEY

"Every time you get into personal contact with Jesus, His words are real. "My peace I give unto you"; it is a peace all over from the crown of the head to the sole of the feet, an irrepressible confidence."

-OSWALD CHAMBERS

The Peace of Knowing Christ

> *[Jesus said,] "You have your heads in your Bibles constantly because you think you'll find eternal life there. But you miss the forest for the trees. These Scriptures are all about me! And here I am, standing right before you, and you aren't willing to receive from me the life you say you want."*
> JOHN 5:39-40 MSG

A. W. Tozer (1897-1963) said, "If there's anything necessary to your eternal happiness but God, you're not the kind of Christian that you ought to be. For only God is the true rest."

When Christians usually think about what divides them from God, they think first of worldly things like money and power. But it is not just worldly things that can divide. Even your relationship with Christ can come between you and Christ.

How can this be? Well, to reach Christ we do many things; we pray, worship, fellowship with believers, read and study the Bible, meditate, fast, and serve others. These outward methods of learning and reaching Christ are good, but they can get in the way. They can distract you from Christ himself. It is quite possible to practice Christian acts of discipline without Christ. We can be so in the routine of reading, studying, and attending church that we miss out on experiencing God himself and allowing Him to change us. We end up not hearing God at all.

Now, this neglect of God is not the same as the desert times when God is silent—during those times our job is to continue obeying and to wait in love for Him to return. Instead, this neglect misses the purpose of prayer and Christian activities altogether. It is easy to miss God's presence and be satisfied with the trappings of the Christian experience. There are many who attend church and study who have always lived like this—without Christ…and without knowing it.

But, oh, what a blessing we miss when we walk in this kind of darkness! The best thing about a Christian life is the awesome reality of God meeting us face-to-face. And He is awesome. He will never meet our earthbound expectations but will exceed them. He will always work for our good. He loves to bless us—mostly with His presence and life-changing power, but also with material gifts and meaningful relationships. He is our Father who loves each of us, our best friend who knows us, and our King who made us.

To seek Him sincerely, we need to wake up from the routine of our religious activities. We need to live with Jesus as a person and ask Him to be real to us.

Ask Him to give you the desire for more than a routine. Then you will find your life with Him easy and at the same time awe-inspiring.

> *Jesus, my only Hope, Jesus, my King,*
> *Help me with heart and voice Thy praise to sing;*
> *Now let Thy beams divine, bright o'er my pathway shine,*
> *Draw me, O Savior mine, closer to Thee.*
> —FANNY CROSBY

The Purpose of Life— to Love God

"Love God, your God, with your whole heart: love him with all that's in you, love him with all you've got!"
DEUTERONOMY 6:5 MSG

When we think of the purpose of life, we typically think of a specific plan created just for us. But often God thinks of a broader purpose for our life on earth that is more important than the specific path. Bernard of Clairvaux (1090-1153) says our purpose is to return God's love. It is that simple, but very important.

"What can I give back to God for the blessings he's poured out on me?" (Psalm 116:12 MSG) Reason and natural fairness both move me to give myself entirely to loving Him—to whom I owe all that I have and am. But faith shows me that I should love Him far more than I love myself, as I come to realize that He has given me not my own life only, but even Himself.

Yet, before the time of full revelation had come, before the Word was made flesh, died on the Cross, came forth from the grave, and returned to His Father; before God had shown us how much He loved us by all this fullness of grace, He gave us the commandment, "You shall love the Lord your God with all your heart and with all your soul, and with all your might"

(Deuteronomy 6:5 NASB). So, love Him with all your being, all your knowledge, and all your powers.

Was it unjust for God to claim this from His own work and gifts? Why shouldn't the creature love his Creator, who gave him the power to love? Why shouldn't we love Him with all our being, since it is by His gift alone that we can do anything that is good? It was God's creative grace that He raised us out of nothingness to the dignity of people; and from this grace appears our duty to love Him, and the justice of His claim to that love. But how infinitely is our reward increased when we think of His fulfillment of the promise, "Your righteousness is like the mighty mountains, your justice like the ocean depths. You care for people and animals alike, O Lord" (Psalm 36:6 NLT).

-BERNARD OF CLAIRVAUX

"God has given you a mind to know Him, a memory to recall His favors, a will to love Him, eyes to see what He does, and a tongue to sing His praise. This is the reason you are here."

-FRANCIS DE SALES, PARAPHRASED BY BERNARD BANGLEY

Peace and Surrender

*"Man looks at the outward appearance,
but the Lord looks at the heart."*
1 SAMUEL 16:7 NASB

Sometimes Christians have difficulty feeling that they are devoted to God fully. We feel as if there is no possible way that we can be as holy as our heroes like Mother Teresa or Billy Graham, let alone Christ himself. All this comparison and self-judgment is negative and damaging. Francois de Fenelon (1651-1715) reassures us that God doesn't measure the amount of love we have for Him but instead looks at whether we are heading towards Him or away from Him.

The ultimate method for inner peace is in the surrender to Christ. Christ wants our all, our entire being; but more than that He wants us to want it too. So when we seek His will, and even in times of inner turmoil when we seek to desire His will, we will find ourselves dwelling in the center of His love.

Remain in peace; the fervor of devotion does not depend upon yourself; all that lies in your power is the direction of your will. Give that up to God without reservation. The important question is not how much you enjoy religion, but whether you will whatever God wills.

Humbly confess your faults. Be detached from the world and abandoned to God. Love Him more than yourself and

His glory more than your life. The least you can do is to desire and ask for such a love. God will then love you and put his peace in your heart.

-FRANCOIS DE FENELON

> *I cannot tell thee whence it came,*
> *This peace within my breast;*
> *But this I know, there fills my soul*
> *A strange and tranquil rest.*
>
> -JOHN S. BROWN

The Purpose of Brokenness

[Jesus said,] "Truly, truly, I say to you, unless a grain of wheat falls into the earth and dies, it remains by itself alone; but if it dies, it bears much fruit."

JOHN 12:24 NASB

No one naturally wants to suffer. No one wants to be broken. However, suffering is a necessary part of the Christian life. It forces us to give up trying to live life on our own strength and instead to rest solely upon God. And when we rely only on God, He then can do miracles through us.

In the following excerpt, Watchman Nee (1903-1972) explains the necessity of brokenness. He uses the terms inner man and outer man. The inner man is the new life, or spirit, that Christ has given us in the Holy Spirit. The outer man is the natural person, or the flesh that comprises the personality and abilities that one is born with.

Anyone who serves God will discover sooner or later that the great hindrance to his work is not others but himself. He will discover that his outward man and his inward man are not in harmony, for both are tending toward opposite directions. He will also sense the inability of his outward man to submit to the spirit's control, thus rendering him incapable of obeying God's highest commands. He will quickly detect that the greatest difficulty lies in his outward man, for it hinders him from using his spirit.

We find the answer to this conflict in the paradoxical statement by Jesus, "He who loves his life loses it; and he who hates his life in this world shall keep it" (John 12:25 NASB). The Lord shows us here that the outer shell is our own life, while the Life within is the eternal Life, which He has given to us with His Spirit. To allow the inner Life to come forth, it is imperative that the outward life be lost. Should the outward remain unbroken, the inward would never be able to come forth.

-WATCHMAN NEE

Light after darkness, gain after loss,
Strength after weakness, crown after cross;
Sweet after bitter, hope after fears,
Home after wandering, praise after tears.
-FRANCES RIDLEY HAVERGAL

Peace in the Assurance of Salvation

Neither height nor depth, nor anything else in all creation, will be able to separate us from the love of God that is in Christ Jesus our Lord.
ROMANS 8:39 NIV

The assurance of salvation and the peace that protects from accusations from the evil one comes only though God. John Bunyan (1628-1688) struggled in a cloud of doubt and depression for years because the knowledge of his own sin and guilt was much stronger than the knowledge of Christ's forgiveness. The following excerpt shows one of several occasions where God demonstrated His love for Bunyan.

I heard one preach a sermon upon those words in Song of Solomon 4:1, "Behold thou art fair, my love; behold, thou art fair" (KJV). He made these two words, "My love," his subject matter. I got nothing out of what he said at first. It was only when he said we are Christ's love when under temptation that I paid attention. He said, "If it is true, that the saved soul is Christ's love when under temptation and desertion; then, poor tempted soul, when you are assaulted and afflicted with temptation, and you feel God hiding His face, think on these two words, 'My love.'"

So as I was going home, these words came again into my thoughts; and I remember I said in my heart, "What shall I get by thinking on these two words?" This thought had no sooner passed through my heart, but these words began to grow in my spirit, Thou art my love, thou art my love, over and over; and still as they ran through my mind, they waxed stronger and warmer, and began to make me look up. But I was still between hoping and fearing, so I wondered, "But is it true, is it true?" At which, the sentence fell in upon me, "He [Peter] did not know that what was being done by the angel was real, but thought he was seeing a vision" (Acts 12:9 NASB).

Then I began to believe the words, which, with power, did over and over make this joyful sound within my soul, Thou art my love, thou art my love; and nothing shall separate you from my love. And with that, Romans 8:39 came into my mind. Now was my heart filled full of comfort and hope, and now I could believe that my sins should be forgiven. Indeed, I was now so taken with the love and mercy of God that I remember I didn't know how I could contain it before I got home. I thought I could have spoken of His love and of His mercy to me, even to the very crows that sat upon the ploughed lands before me.

-JOHN BUNYAN

Peace in God's Presence

[Job replied to the Lord:] " Surely I spoke of things I did not understand, things too wonderful for me to know. . . . My ears had heard of you but now my eyes have seen you."

JOB 42:3,5 NIV

When bad things happen there will be blessings. We will change, grow, or receive comfort. We will know God more. Even Job who lost family, possessions, reputation, and health was ultimately blessed by God's presence. He shouted and complained at God for an explanation for his circumstances and his pain. The answer Job received instead was no explanation, only the magnificent presence of God. And that was sufficient.

All was taken away and replaced by the only thing important—God himself. This intimate knowledge of God made all of his suffering and all of his questions immaterial. The material blessings that followed in Job's life were just a token of God's love and approval. Job had already received what he wanted—God.

"Whenever His hand is laid upon you, it is ineffable peace and comfort, the sense that 'Underneath are the everlasting arms,' full of sustaining and comfort and strength."

-OSWALD CHAMBERS

God's Purpose for Trials

"See, I lay a stone in Zion, a tested stone, a precious cornerstone for a sure foundation; the one who trusts will never be dismayed."
ISAIAH 28:16 NIV

The only way for us to rely on God alone is to recognize our need for Him in everything. Hannah Whitall Smith (1832-1911) writes that trials and storms come to shake us off of our flimsy and false foundations and cause us to stand on the strong foundation of God that will never fail.

Often the Lord sees that we are building our spiritual lives on flimsy foundations that will not be able to withstand the storms of life. In tender love, He shakes our earth and our heaven until all that can be shaken is removed, and only those things that cannot be shaken are left behind.

Paul tells us that the things that are shaken are the "things that are made." These are things manufactured by our own efforts, feelings that we work up, doctrines that we invent, and good works that we perform. It is not that these are bad things in themselves. It is only when the soul begins to rest on them instead of upon the Lord that He is compelled to shake us from them.

There are times in our Christian lives when our faith seems to be as settled and immovable as the roots of the everlasting mountains. But then comes an upheaval, and all our foundations are shaken and thrown down. We are ready to despair and question whether we can be Christians at all.

The upheaval may come in our outward circumstances. Everything seems so firmly established in prosperity that no dream of disaster disturbs us. Our reputation is assured, our work has prospered, our efforts have all been successful beyond our hopes, and our soul is at ease. The need for God is in danger of becoming far off and vague.

Then the Lord is obliged to put an end to it all. Our prosperity crumbles around us like a house built on the sand. We are tempted to think He is angry with us. But in truth, it is not anger, but tender love. His love compels Him to take away the outward prosperity that is keeping our souls from the true peace and joy that comes from a relationship with Christ.

God uses trials to drive us directly to Him. He longs to be our everything. Nothing else in this world will satisfy our soul.

-HANNAH WHITALL SMITH

> *Christ is our Cornerstone,*
> *On Him alone we build;*
> *On His great love our hopes we place*
> *Of present grace and joys above.*
>
> -UNKNOWN AUTHOR, SIXTH CENTURY,
> TRANSLATED BY JOHN CHANDLER

The Purpose of Holiness

*Consecrate yourselves therefore, and be holy;
for I am the Lord your God.*
LEVITICUS 20:7 AMP

The way to purity and holiness is Christ. Only He can cancel sin and improve character. The Bible commentary writer Adam Clarke (1715-1832) writes that the way to see God and know Him is through being holy like Christ.

No faith or belief in any particular creed, no religious observance, no obedience to laws and rules, no acts of benevolence and charity, and no humiliation or remorse can be a substitute for purification. We must be made part of the divine nature of God. We must be saved from our sins—from the corruption that is in the world—and be holy within and righteous without, or never see God in His holiness and perfection.

For this very purpose Jesus Christ lived, died, and rose again, that He might purify us unto himself; that through faith in His blood our sins might be blotted out, and our souls restored to the image of God.

Are you hungering and thirsting after righteousness? Then, you are blessed, for you shall be filled.

-ADAM CLARKE

Peace in Submission

*[Jesus said,] "Peace I leave with you, My peace I give to you;
not as the world gives do I give to you."*
JOHN 14:27 NKJV

In the following entry, Thomas à Kempis (1379-1471) writes that true peace is found in submission. The servant leadership that Jesus modeled depended upon following the will of God no matter what our own desires are. And when we follow God's will, He will respond with the gifts of peace and growth.

God's peace is with the humble and meek of heart: your peace will be found in much patience. If you hear Christ and follow His voice, you will be able to enjoy much peace.

First, watch yourself in all things, in what you do and what you say. Direct your every intention toward pleasing God alone, and desire nothing outside of God. Do not be quick to judge the deeds and words of others, and do not entangle yourself in affairs that are not your own. Thus, it will come about that you will be disturbed little and seldom.

Then realize that the lack of conflict is not the presence of peace. Do not think that you have found true peace if you feel no depression, or that all is well because you suffer no opposition. Do not think that all is perfect if everything happens just as you wish. And do not imagine yourself great or consider yourself especially beloved if you are filled with great love and sweetness. For the progress and perfection of a Christian does not consist in a life of ease.

Instead, spiritual growth consists in offering yourself with all your heart to God's will, not seeking what is yours either in small matters or great ones, either in temporary or eternal things.

In brief, seek to do the will of others rather than your own. Always choose to have less rather than more. Look always for the last place and seek to be beneath all others. Always wish and pray that the will of God be fully carried out in you. Then you will enter into the realm of peace and rest.

-Thomas à Kempis

Purpose in Prayer

"I have heard your prayers and seen your tears; I will heal you."
2 KINGS 20:5 NIV

God in His amazing love is a relational God. He wants us to talk to Him—to tell Him what we care about and ask Him for what we want. He enjoys responding to our prayers and changing our situations. He loves us, and that love transcends all boundaries. He gives us power in prayer. We can move mountains when we submit to Him. E. M. Bounds (1835-1913) writes of the benefits of prayer to the individual and to the world.

The more praying there is in the world the better the world will be. Prayer, in one phase of its operation, is a disinfectant and a preventive. It purifies the air; it destroys the contagion of evil. Prayer is no fitful, short-lived thing. It is no voice crying unheard and unheeded in the silence. It is a voice which goes into God's ear, and it lives as long as God's ear is open to holy pleas, as long as God's heart is alive to holy things.

The one who has done the most and the best praying is the most immortal. They are God's heroes, God's saints, God's servants, God's commanders. A person can pray better because of the prayers of the past; a person can live holier because of the prayers of the past; the person of many prayers has done the truest and greatest service to the incoming generation.

The prayers of God's saints strengthen the unborn generation against the desolating waves of sin and evil. Woe to the generation of children who find their censers empty of the rich incense of prayer; whose parents have been too busy or too unbelieving to pray, and perils inexpressible and consequences untold are their unhappy heritage. Fortunate are they whose fathers and mothers have left them a wealthy patrimony of prayer.

-E. M. BOUNDS

"To suppose that God and the individual communicate... and that because of the interchange God does what he had not previously intended, or refrains from something he previously had intended to do, is nothing against God's dignity if it is an arrangement he himself has chosen."

-DALLAS WILLARD

Peace of Mind

God doesn't stir us up into confusion; he brings us into harmony.
1 CORINTHIANS 14:33 MSG

Quite often when we pray, we get distracted. We want to focus on Jesus, our Lord and friend, but instead we find ourselves discouraged and distracted. Random thoughts enter our head. We have trouble concentrating. These thoughts can be entertaining, worrying, or plain disgusting. It can be hard to overcome them and to be at peace in prayer.

When you are praying and a distracting thought enters your mind, don't fight it. Let it flow past. Imagine the thought as a boat going down a stream. If you fight the thought, you are trying to push the boat back up the stream. You will end up spending all your energy trying to keep it out of your mind. When you tire, the boat will naturally come downstream and enter your mind again. Instead of fighting it, let the thought flow on past you down the stream. It will go through your mind and you may notice it momentarily, but then it will be gone. You are then free to focus on God.

The Purpose of Silent Prayer

O God, we meditate on your unfailing love.
PSALM 48:9 NIV

When we are silent in prayer, we learn to ignore our own thoughts and to listen to God. Walter Hilton (1340-1396) writes of how silent prayer leads to an understanding of who God is.

If you ever seek with great diligence in prayer you will come to a sight of God. Then you may know the wisdom of God, the endless might of Him, His great goodness in himself and in His creatures. This is contemplation [that is, silent prayer in which you spend time just being with God]. It is just like Paul said, "I pray that you, being rooted and established in love, may have power, together with all the saints, to grasp how wide and long and high and deep is the love of Christ" (Ephesians 3:17-18 NIV).

He did not say that you may know by a sound in your ear nor a flavor in your mouth, nor by any of your natural senses, but that you may know and feel with all saints what is the length of the endless being of God, the breadth of the wonderful charity and the goodness of God, the height of His almighty Majesty and the bottomless depths of His wisdom. Knowing and feeling these things should be the purpose of a praying Christian. For in these may be understood the full knowing of all spiritual things.

I shall stretch out my heart ever forward for to feel and to grip the sovereign reward of endless bliss.

-WALTER HILTON

Silent Prayer—Focusing on God Alone

As for me, it is good to be near God.
PSALM 73:28 NIV

The method of silent prayer can be very useful in dwelling in the peace of God. King David said it is better to spend one day in His courts than thousands elsewhere. (See Psalm 84:10.) The following exercise in silent prayer comes from the early Christian classic, *Cloud of Unknowing*. It offers simple directions on focusing your heart on God and glorifying Him with the decision to rest in His presence.

Lift up your heart to God with a meek stirring of love; and focus on Him and none of His gifts. And then, seek to think on nothing but Him. So that nothing is at work in your mind, nor in your will, but only Him. And do what you can to forget all the creatures that God made and what they have accomplished; so that neither your thought nor your desire be directed nor stretched to any of them, neither in general nor in special, but let them be, and pay no attention to them.

This is the work of the soul that pleases God the most, to focus solely on Him. All saints and angels have joy of this work, and they hurry to help it with all their might. All fiends are furious when you do this, and try to defeat it in all that they can.

-AUTHOR UNKNOWN

Preserving Peace in Love

"Beloved, let us love one another, for love is of God."
1 JOHN 4:7 NKJV

It is much easier for us to bear up under insults and deal with conflict in love when we consider the love God has for our friends. He does not love us more than them. He created them in His image also. The easiest way to begin is to pray for them. Pray that they may be blessed, and they will be blessed—but so will we.

There are three things that are essential to helping us preserve both inward and outward peace. One of these is love for each other; the second, detachment from all created things; the third, true humility.

With regard to the first—namely, love for each other—this is of very great importance; for there is nothing, however annoying, that cannot easily be borne by those who love each other, and anything which causes annoyance must be quite exceptional. If this commandment were kept in the world, as it should be, I believe it would take us a long way towards the keeping of the rest.

-TERESA OF AVILA (1515-1582)

When we pray for our friends, our understanding and love for them will grow. As our love increases, so will our ability to patiently forgive them and work towards peace.

Purpose to Know Yourself

*Make a careful exploration of who you are and the work
you have been given, and then sink yourself into that.
Don't be impressed with yourself.
Don't compare yourself with others.*
GALATIANS 6:4 MSG

The philosopher Socrates was the first person to say that to know yourself is the beginning of all knowledge. This applies both physically and spiritually. However, philosophers believe that rational thought is the only method to self-knowledge. The Bible teaches that God is the way of all wisdom.

Psalm 139 NIV begins, "O Lord, you have searched me and you know me". To achieve self-knowledge, like the following passage recommends, we should seek God and His understanding of us.

It is good and profitable that we should ask, learn, and know, what good and holy men have done and suffered, and how God has dealt with them, and what He has done in and through them. However, it is a thousand times better that we should learn and perceive and understand in ourselves who we are, how and what our own life is, what God is and is doing in us, what He will have from us, and to what ends He will or will not make use of us.

For to know oneself thoroughly is a high skill. If you know

yourself well, you are better and more worthy of praise before God, than if you instead understand the course of the heavens and of all the planets and stars, also the dispositions of all people, also the nature of all animals, and, in such matters, had all the skill of all who are in heaven and on earth.

-THEOLOGICA GERMANICA, UNKNOWN 16TH CENTURY AUTHOR

"Lord Jesus, Let me know myself and know You, and desire nothing save You."

-AUGUSTINE OF HIPPO (354-430)

How to Seek and Maintain Peace

May the God of hope fill you with all joy and peace in believing, that you may abound in hope by the power of the Holy Spirit.
ROMANS 15:13 NKJV

Peace is a gift from God. It is one of the fruits of the Spirit. We need not manufacture peace in ourselves, but we must receive it and give it room to flourish and grow. According to Thomas Watson (1620-1686), the ways to seek and maintain peace are to nourish faith, seek Christian fellowship, see only the good in others, and to pray for the spirit of peace to overflow our lives.

Let us labor for the things that maintain and cherish peace.

Live in faith. Faith and peace keep a house together. Faith believes the Word of God. The Word says, "Live in peace" (2 Corinthians 13:11 NIV). And as soon as faith sees the King of heaven's warrant, it obeys. Faith persuades the soul that God is at peace, and it is impossible to believe this and live in conflict. Nourish faith. Faith knits us to God in love and to our fellow Christians in peace.

Seek regular Christian communion. There should not be too much distance between Christians. The primitive saints had their "agapai," that is, love feasts. The apostle, exhorting us to peace, gives us a practical application: "Be kind and compassionate to one another" (Ephesians 4:32 NIV).

Do not look upon the failings of others, but upon their graces. There is no perfection here. We read of the "spot of God's children" (Deuteronomy 32:5 KJV). The most golden Christians are some grains too light. Oh, let us not so quarrel with the infirmities of others and pass by their virtues. If in some things they fail, in other things they excel. It is the manner of the world to look more upon the sun in an eclipse than when it shines in its full bright glory.

Pray to God that He will send down the Spirit of peace into our hearts. We should not as vultures prey one upon another, but pray one for another.

Pray that God will quench the fire of contention and kindle the fire of compassion in our hearts one to another.

-Thomas Watson

God's Will

> *When Christ came into the world, he said: "Sacrifice and offering you did not desire, but a body you prepared for me . . . I have come to do your will, O God."*
> HEBREWS 10:5, 7 NIV

What is God's will? Are we supposed to serve at every event and on every committee? If someone asks for our involvement, do we have to say yes to be good servants and good Christians? A wise person once said, "There are many good things for you to do, but do the few things He tells you to do." The following excerpt by Alphonsus di Ligouri (1696-1787) points us in the right direction of serving God and learning about His will for our life.

The principal effect of love is so to unite the wills of those who love each other as to make their will the same. It follows then, that the more one unites his will with God's will, the greater will be his love of God. Dying to self, thinking long and deep about God's principles and Christ's life, receiving Communion, and acts of charity are all certainly pleasing to God—but only when they are in accordance with His will. When they do not agree with God's will, He not only finds no pleasure in them, but He rejects them utterly.

To illustrate this concept is the following story: A man has two servants. One works non-stop all day but according to his own devices. The other, conceivably, works less, but he does what he is told. The second of course is going to find favor in the eyes of his master; the other will not.

The prophet Samuel told King Saul, "What is more pleasing to the Lord: your burnt offerings and sacrifices or your obedience to his voice? Obedience is far better than sacrifice. Listening to him is much better than offering the fat of rams" (1 Samuel 15:22 NLT). The one who follows their own will independently of God's is guilty of a kind of idolatry. Instead of adoring God's will, they, in a certain sense, adore their own.

The greatest glory we can give to God is to listen and do His will in everything. Our Redeemer came on earth to glorify His heavenly Father and to teach us by His example how to do the same.

-ALPHONSUS DI LIGOURI

We should not worry about trying to please everyone. Instead, we should try to please God. And this is not a difficult task. God desires our love and companionship as much as He desires our obedience. As we seek to do His will, we will find it easier to accomplish.

The Purpose of Guilt

God can use sorrow in our lives to help us turn away from sin and seek salvation. We will never regret that kind of sorrow. But sorrow without repentance is the kind that results in death.

2 CORINTHIANS 7:10 NLT

The closer we grow to God, the more His glory and perfection shines, and in turn, our own sense of unworthiness expands. If we are not followers of Christ, then this sense of conviction leads us to find the redemption and forgiveness He offers. The light of Christ's beauty reveals the dirty stains and smudges on what we thought before was our white and clean life. This sense of conviction has a purpose. Even in the mature Christian life, guilt can play a major part in moving us closer to God. It leads to a changed life, one that models the perfect Christ. Richard Baxter shows how the misery of our conviction of sin turns to joy with the gift of mercy from God.

God's goodness convinces the Christian of the evil of sin. We sinners are made to know and feel that the sin which was our delight is a more loathsome thing than a toad or serpent, and a greater evil than plague or famine because it is a breach of the righteous law of the most high God, dishonorable to Him and destructive to us. Now we don't only hear the accusation of sin in words; but the mention of our sin speaks to our heart. . . . We used to marvel what made people get worked up against sin. We could see no real harm for a person to take a little forbidden pleasure. Now the case is altered; God has opened our eyes to see the inexpressible vileness of sin, especially in our own life.

We are then convinced of our own misery because of sin. We who before read the threats of God's law as people do the stories of foreign wars, now find it our own story, and perceive we read our own doom, as if we found our own names written in the curses of the Bible. The wrath of God seemed to us before but a storm to a person safe in a dry house, or as the pains of the sick to the healthful bystander. But now we find the disease is our own and feel ourselves condemned: that we are dead and damned in point of law, and that nothing is wanting but mere execution to make us absolutely and irrecoverably miserable.

This is a work of the Spirit wrought in some measure in all the regenerate. How should we come to Christ for pardon if we did not first find ourselves guilty and condemned? Or how can we come to Christ for life, if we never found ourselves spiritually dead? "It is not the healthy who need a doctor, but the sick" (Mark 2:17 NIV). The discovery of the remedy in Christ after the misery of sin and guilt take over is a truly joyous occasion. And perhaps the joyful anticipation of mercy may make the sense of misery in guilt soon forgotten.

-RICHARD BAXTER

Dear children, continue in him, so that when he appears we may be confident and unashamed before him at his coming.

1 JOHN 2:28 NIV

THE PEACE OF CHRIST

*Grace and peace to you from God our Father and
the Lord Jesus Christ.*
ROMANS 1:7 NIV

The common greeting of "Grace and peace to you" is simple and yet contains great encouragement and strength for Christ's followers. In his commentary on Galatians, Martin Luther (1483-1546) explains the miraculous nature of the peace of Christ.

The Apostle Paul wishes to the Galatians grace and peace, not from the emperor, or kings and princes: for those commonly persecute the godly, and rise up against the Lord, and Christ His anointed. (See Psalm 2:2.) This grace and peace is also not from the world because "In this world," said Christ, "you will have trouble" (John 16:33 NIV). But grace and peace is from God our Father, which is as much to say, Paul wished for them a heavenly peace.

So Christ said, "I have told you these things, so that in me you may have peace. In this world you will have trouble. But take heart! I have overcome the world" (John 16:33 NIV). The peace of the world grants nothing but the peace of our goods and bodies. So the grace or favor of the world gives us leave to enjoy our goods, and casts us not out of our possessions. But in affliction and in the hour of death, the grace and favor of the world cannot help us; they cannot deliver us from affliction, despair, and death.

But when the grace and peace of God are in the heart, then we are strong, so that we can neither be cast down with adversity, nor puffed up with prosperity, but walk on plainly, and keep the highway. For we take heart and courage in the victory of Christ's death. The confidence of this begins to reign in our conscience over sin and death; because, through Him, we have assured forgiveness of our sins; which after we have once obtained our conscience is at rest, and by the word of grace is comforted. So then when we are comforted and heartened by the grace of God (that is, by forgiveness of sin, and by this peace of conscience), we are able valiantly to bear and overcome all troubles, yes, even death itself.

-MARTIN LUTHER

One of the most peaceful images of our relationship with God is that of the Good Shepherd with His sheep. The poet George Herbert's version of Psalm 23 emphasizes how the peaceful Shepherd provides.

> *He leads me to the tender grasse,*
> *Where I both feed and rest:*
> *Then to the streams that gently passe:*
> *In both I have the best.*
> -GEORGE HERBERT (1593-1633)

Jesus' Purpose

*This is how God showed his love among us:
He sent his one and only Son into the world that we
might live through him.*

1 JOHN 4:9 NIV

What was Jesus' purpose? He had many opportunities to follow a different career path. He could have been a carpenter, a preacher, a magician, a revolutionary leader, or even a king or emperor. Although He had the power to do all these things, Jesus was first a sacrifice.

He walked through life obedient at every turn. He never lost focus or stayed too long in one place. Step by step He followed a path that no one else could see. He knew that the purpose of His life was death and resurrection—to be a sacrifice so that we too could live free from sin and spend eternity with God.

There are many who think that to dwell on Christ's death and the cross isn't necessary—that to dwell on the pain He suffered and the sacrifice He made is morbid. And it would be, except for the truth of the Resurrection. Jesus died, and then He rose again. That is the point.

He rose again and lives still. His purpose is life, and life eternal—for us and for Him. So when we think of His life as a model, and we consider the sacrifice He made and the death He went through, this is the same as what we as Christians go through. We give up our life, die to our sins, and rise again, empowered and free.

Once we are aware that Christ gave up everything for us because of His love for us, we can then follow steadily after Him. There is nothing holding us back. We have love, we have power, and we have freedom!

The Purpose of Pruning

*My Father . . . cuts away every branch of mine that doesn't produce fruit.
But he trims clean every branch that does produce fruit,
so that it will produce even more fruit.*

JOHN 15:1-2 CEV

In the whole plant world, only the vine is perfectly suited as an example of the relationship between God and His people. Of all plants, not one needs the pruning knife so unsparingly and so unceasingly as the vine. The Savior, with a single word, refers to this need of pruning in the vine and the blessing it brings: "But he trims clean every branch that does produce fruit, so that it will produce even more fruit."

And so He has prepared His people to hear in each affliction the voice of a messenger that comes to call them to abide still more closely. Yes, believer, especially in times of trial, abide in Christ.

In the storm, the tree strikes deeper roots in the soil; in the hurricane the inhabitants of the house abide within and rejoice in its shelter. So in the midst of our suffering, the Father would lead us to enter more deeply into the love of Christ. Our hearts are continually prone to wander from Him; prosperity and enjoyment all too easily satisfy us.

"Pray for grace to see in every trouble, small or great, the Father's finger pointing to Jesus, and saying, Abide in Him."

-ANDREW MURRAY (1828-1917)

God Is a God of Peace

Grace and peace to you from God our Father and from the Lord Jesus Christ.
ROMANS 1:7 NIV

God is a God of peace and of love. He lives in unity with the Son and the Spirit. This unity and peace is offered to us in our relationship with Christ. Thomas Watson tells us that God's name is peace. If we long for peace, then we long for God.

God the Father is called "the God of peace" (Hebrews 13:20 NIV). Mercy and peace are about His throne. He signs the articles of peace and sends the ambassadors of peace to publish them. (See 2 Corinthians 5:20.)

God the Son is called "the Prince of Peace" (Isaiah 9:6 NASB). His name is Emmanuel, God with us, a name of peace. His office is to be a mediator of peace. (See 1 Timothy 2:5.) He came into the world with a song of peace; the angels sang it: "Peace on earth" (Luke 2:14 NLT). He went out of the world with a legacy of peace: "Peace I leave with you, My peace I give to you" (John 14:27 NKJV).

God the Holy Ghost is a Spirit of peace. He is the Comforter. He seals up peace (2 Corinthians 1:22). This blessed dove brings the olive branch of peace in His mouth. Now a peaceable disposition gives evidence of God in a person. Therefore God loves to dwell there. "In Salem also is God's tabernacle" (Psalm 76:2 NKJV). Salem means "peace." God dwells in a peaceable spirit.

-THOMAS WATSON

The Purpose of Purity

God disciplines us for our good, that we may share in his holiness.
No discipline seems pleasant at the time, but painful. Later on,
however, it produces a harvest of righteousness and peace for
those who have been trained by it.

HEBREWS 12:10-11 NIV

The way to purity isn't easy. It usually involves suffering. However, as St. Catherine of Genoa (1447-1510) wrote, purity is worthwhile because a pure heart is open and free to receive God's love and attention.

"It is," she [St. Catherine of Genoa] says, "as with a covered object, the object cannot respond to the rays of the sun, not because the sun ceases to shine—for it shines without intermission—but because the covering intervenes. Let the covering be destroyed, and again the object will be exposed to the sun, and will answer to the rays that beat against it in proportion as the work of destruction advances.

Likewise the souls are covered by rust—that is, by sin—which is gradually consumed away by the fire of suffering. The more it is consumed, the more they respond to God, their true Sun. Their happiness increases as the rust falls off and lays them open to the divine ray . . . the instinctive tendency to seek happiness in God develops itself, and goes on increasing through the fire of love, which draws it to its end with such impetuosity and vehemence that any obstacle seems intolerable; and the more clear its vision, the more extreme its pain."

EVELYN UNDERHILL

When times of suffering come, we can stay hopeful because as God clears away the sins and distractions in our life, we can see Him and know Him more clearly. As we are able to spend more time in His presence, His presence alone will more than make up for the temporary pain we face. Let us be encouraged rather than anxious when problems and suffering appear in our future. God is good. He longs to teach us more about Him, be with us through our pain, and bless us more than we ever will know. And His greatest blessing has always been himself. As we are purified, we will see Him face-to-face.

Look Up for Peace

Jesus answered, "I am the way and the truth and the life."
JOHN 14:6 NIV

True peace can come only from God. If we trust in ourselves or in others, we will be let down, hurt, and disappointed. It is only when we trust in God and His promises that we will find peace and hope. D. L. Moody (1837-1899), who spent hours daily in prayer with God, tells us that when we focus on God, we will never lose our way.

Someone has said: "There are three ways to look. If you want to be wretched, look within; if you wish to be distracted, look around; but if you would have peace, look up."

Peter looked away from Christ, and he immediately began to sink. The Master said to him, "O you of little faith, why did you doubt?" (Matthew 14:31 NKJV).

He had God's eternal word, which was sure footing, and better than marble, granite, or iron; but the moment he took his eyes off Christ, down he went. Those who look around cannot see how unstable and dishonoring their walk is. We want to look straight at the "Author and Finisher of our faith" (Hebrews 12:2 NKJV).

When I was a boy I could only make a straight track in the snow by keeping my eyes fixed upon a tree or some object before me. The moment I took my eye off the mark set in front of me, I walked crookedly. It is only when we look fixedly on Christ that we find perfect peace. After He rose from the dead He showed His disciples His hands and His feet. "Behold My hands and My feet, that it is I Myself. Handle Me and see, for a spirit does not have flesh and bones as you see I have" (Luke 24:39 NKJV). That was the ground of their peace.

If you want to scatter your doubts, look at the blood; and if you want to increase your doubts, look at yourself. You will get doubts enough for years after being occupied with yourself for only a few days. Then again: look at what He is, and at what He has done; not at what you are, and what you have done. That is the way to get peace and rest.

-D. L. MOODY

Are you aweary?
Does the way seem long?
Look to the Lamb of God
His love will cheer
And fill your heart with song.
Look to the Lamb of God.

-HENRY G. JACKSON

Pray for Peace

Pray for the peace of Jerusalem.
PSALM 122:6 NIV

We are told to pray because prayer changes things—both people and God. E. M. Bounds explains that just as we become more like God as we pray, so also will those we pray for.

We are to pray for all people, but to pray especially for rulers in Church and state, that we "may lead a quiet and peaceable life in all godliness and honesty" (1 Timothy 2:2 KJV). Peace on the outside and peace on the inside. Praying calms disturbing forces, allays tormenting fears, brings conflict to an end. Prayer tends to do away with turmoil.

But even if there be external conflicts, it is well to have deep peace within the citadel of the soul. "That we may lead a quiet and peaceable life." Prayer brings inner calm and furnishes outward tranquility. If praying rulers and praying subjects were worldwide, they would allay turbulent forces, make wars to cease, and peace to reign. We must pray for all people that we may lead lives "in all godliness and honesty"—that is, with godliness and gravity.

Godliness is to be like God. It is to be godly, to have God—likeness, having the image of God stamped upon the inner nature, and showing the same likeness in conduct and in temper. Almighty God is the very highest model, and to be like Him is to possess the highest character. Prayer molds us into the image of God; and at the same time tends to mold others into the same image just in proportion as we pray for them.

-E. M. BOUNDS

The Peace of God's Firm Foundation

The Lord . . . is the Rock eternal.
ISAIAH 26:4 NIV

God is solid. When we focus on Him and His attributes, we will not stumble, but will remain strong and able to face the fiercest challenges. Charles Spurgeon (1834-1892) urges us to turn to God, take refuge in His goodness, and rise up higher than eagles in His presence.

I am not afraid that anyone, who thinks worthily about the Creator, stands in awe of His delightful perfections, and sees Him sitting upon the throne, doing all things according to the counsel of His will, will go far wrong in their doctrinal sentiments. They may say, "My heart is fixed, O God" (Psalm 57:7 KJV). For when the heart is fixed with a firm conviction of the greatness, the omnipotence, the divinity indeed of Him whom we call God, the head will not wander far from truth.

Another happy result of such meditation is the steady peace, the grateful calm it gives to the soul. Have you been a long time at sea, and has the continual motion of the ship sickened and disturbed you? Have you come to look upon everything as moving till you scarcely put one foot before the other without the fear of falling down because the floor rocks beneath your tread? With what delight do you put your feet at last upon the shore and say, "Ah! This does not move; this is solid ground. Even though the tempest howls, this island is safely moored. She will not start from her bearings; when I tread on her she will not yield beneath my feet."

Just so is it with us when we turn from the ever-shifting, often boisterous tide of earthly things to take refuge in the Eternal God who has been "our dwelling-place in all generations" (Psalm 90:1 KJV). The fleeting things of human life, and the fickle thoughts and showy deeds of men, are as moveable and changeable as the waters of the treacherous deep; but when we mount up, as it were, with eagles' wings to Him that sits upon the circle of the earth, before whom all its inhabitants are as grasshoppers, we nestle in the Rock of ages, which from its eternal socket never starts, and in its fixed immovability never can be disturbed.

-REV. C. H. SPURGEON

Rock of Ages, cleft for me,
Let me hide myself in Thee.
-AUGUSTUS M. TOPLADY

The Purpose of Dry Times

My soul thirsts for You; My flesh longs for You in a dry and thirsty land where there is no water. So I have looked for You in the sanctuary, to see Your power and Your glory.
PSALM 63:1-2 NKJV

In the hard times when we feel that God has forsaken us, we instead grow closer and become more like Him. Just as in winter, when the cold temperature and harsh wind strip the flowers and leaves from trees, they give the plants time to focus on necessary root growth. These times may not feel good, but they are vitally important. John of the Cross (1542-1591) wrote of the desert or night times as the time to strip away distractions and to really see God.

In order to prove more completely how this night with its aridity and its desolation is effective in bringing the soul that light which, as we say, it receives there from God, we shall quote that passage of David, where he clearly describes the great power which is in this night for bringing the soul this high knowledge of God. He says, "In the desert land, waterless, dry and pathless, I appeared before Thee, that I might see Thy virtue and Thy glory."

It is an amazing thing that David should say here that the means and the preparation for his knowledge of the glory of God were not from the spiritual delights and the many pleasures he had experienced, but from the dryness and detachments of his sensual nature—the time of dry and desert land.

In this dry condition, again, souls become submissive and obedient upon the spiritual road. For, when they see their own misery, not only do they hear what is taught them, but they even desire that anyone may set them on the way and tell them what they ought to do. The strong belief which they sometimes had in their prosperity is taken from them; and finally, all the other imperfections, the main one being spiritual pride, are swept away from them on this road.

-SAINT JOHN OF THE CROSS

> *Fill me with gladness from above,*
> *Hold me by strength divine;*
> *Lord, make the glow of Thy great love*
> *Through my whole being shine.*
>
> -JOHANN C. LAVATER,
> TRANSLATED BY ELIZABETH L. SMITH

Peace and a Good Conscience

*Humble yourselves in the sight of the Lord,
and He will lift you up.*
JAMES 4:10 NKJV

The way to internal peace is a conscience that is clean before God. When we humble ourselves, admit our wrongs, and seek God's glory, we will discover the beauty of His peace. John Bunyan describes the difference humility and a clean conscience make in our lives. God will lift up the humble. We will rise on wings like eagles.

The person that has a good conscience to God, has a continual feast in their own soul: while others say there is casting down, they shall say there is lifting up—for God shall save the humble person.

Some indeed, in the midst of their profession, are reproached, smitten, and condemned by their own heart. Their conscience is still biting and stinging them because of the uncleanness of their hands. They cannot lift up their face unto God because they have not the answer of a good conscience towards Him, but must walk as persons false to their God and as traitors to their own eternal welfare.

But the godly, upright person shall have the light shine upon their path, and they shall take their steps in butter and honey. The work of righteousness shall be peace, and the effect of righteousness, quietness, and assurance forever. "For if our heart condemns us, God is greater than our heart, and knows all things. Beloved, if our heart does not condemn us, we have confidence toward God" (1 John 3:20-21 NKJV).

-JOHN BUNYAN

> *Let not conscience make you linger,*
> *Not of fitness fondly dream;*
> *All the fitness He requires*
> *Is to feel your need of Him.*
>
> -JOSEPH HART

Purpose to Pray

*Evening and morning and at noon I will pray, and cry aloud,
and He shall hear my voice.*
PSALM 55:17 NKJV

What advice would you give to your children, or even your grandchildren? The founder of the Quakers, William Penn (1644-1718), wrote a book of advice to his spiritual children and to his actual children. He stressed the importance of focusing on God from the start, early in the morning before you get distracted by the tasks of the day.

I will begin here also with the beginning of time—the morning. So, as soon as you wake, retire your mind into a pure silence from all thoughts and ideas of worldly things. In that frame of mind wait upon God, to feel His good presence, to lift up your hearts to Him, and commit your whole self into His blessed care and protection.

Then rise immediately if you are well. Once dressed, read a chapter or more in the Scriptures, and afterwards dispose yourselves for the business of the day. Always remember that God is present and the overseer of all your thoughts, words, and actions, and humble yourselves accordingly. Don't you dare to do anything in His holy, all-seeing presence, which you would be ashamed another—even a child—should see you do. And as you have intervals from your lawful occasions, delight to step home (within yourselves, I mean), commune with your own heart and be still.

-WILLIAM PENN

"The dew comes down when all nature is at rest—when every leaf is still. A calm hour with God is worth a whole lifetime with man."

-ROBERT MURRAY M'CHEYNE

God's Purposes Cannot Be Frustrated

Many, O Lord my God, are the wonders you have done. The things you planned for us no one can recount to you; were I to speak and tell of them, they would be too many to declare.
PSALM 40:5 NIV

Christians have often struggled with the dual concepts of predestination and free will. Does God choose us to be believers, or do we choose to follow Him? How can God let us choose to love Him if He is all powerful and in control of the world? Charles Spurgeon decides the answer is both predestination and free will. It may be hard to grasp, but the majesty of God usually is.

O Christians, you shall never be able to comprehend this, but you may wonder at it. I know there is an easy way of getting out of this great deep, either by denying predestination altogether or by denying free-will altogether, but if you can hold the two, if you can say, "Yes, my consciousness teaches me that man does as he wills, but my faith teaches me that God does as He wills, and these two are not contrary the one to the other; and yet I cannot tell how it is, I cannot tell how God effects His end, I can only wonder and admire, and say, 'Oh, the depth of the riches both of the wisdom and knowledge of God! How unsearchable are His judgments and His ways past finding out!'" (Romans 11:33 NKJV).

Every creature is free and doing as it wills, yet God is more free still and doing as He wills, not only in heaven but among the inhabitants of this lower earth. I have therefore given you a general subject upon which I would invite you to spend your meditations in your quiet hours, for I am persuaded that sometimes to think of these deep doctrines will be found very profitable. It will be to you like the advice of Christ to Simon Peter: "Launch out into the deep and let down your nets for a catch" (Luke 5:4 NKJV).

You shall have a catch of exceeding great thoughts and exceeding great graces if you dare to launch out into this exceeding deep sea, and let out the nets of your contemplation at the command of Christ. "Behold, God is great." "O LORD, how great are Your works! Your thoughts are very deep!" (Psalm 92:5 NKJV).

-C. H. SPURGEON

> "[God] is unique and who can turn Him?
> And what His soul desires, that He does."
>
> JOB 23:13 NASB

God's Amazing Purpose

> *We know that God causes all things to work together for good to those who love God, to those who are called according to His purpose.*
> ROMANS 8:28 NASB

It may be hard for even the believer to remember that God is in control and His will is perfect when pain and suffering and evil often triumph. In his sermon, "The Infallibility of God's Purpose," Charles Spurgeon insists that God is good and is not in charge of our suffering.

Now, the fact taught here is, that in all the acts of God in Providence, He has a fixed and a settled purpose. "He is in one mind" (Job 23:13 KJV). It is a consolation to us who are God's creatures, to know that He did not make us without a purpose, and that now, in all His dealings with us, He has the same wise and gracious end to be served.

Spurgeon goes on to name the problems Christians face in the world: suffering, hard work with no results, and the death of good people. These problems are not in control, but under the control of God's love and goodness. God protects us from much suffering, but when He lets bad things happen, He remains with us, comforts us, and continues working so that only blessings will come to us in the end.

Spurgeon encourages us with the following:

O believer, ever look, then, on all your sufferings as being parts of the divine plan, and say, as wave upon wave rolls over you, "He is in one mind!" He is carrying out still His one great purpose; none of this comes by chance, none of this happens to us out of order, but everything comes to us according to the purpose of His own will, and answers the purpose of His own great mind.

In conclusion, Spurgeon says, "From every evil, good has come," reminding us of the blessings that resulted from Christ's suffering on the cross and similarly how the suffering of Christians often furthers the kingdom of God.

From every evil good has come, and the more the evil has accumulated, the more God has glorified himself in bringing out at last His grand, His everlasting design. This is the first general lesson of the text—in every event of Providence, God has a purpose. "He is in one mind."

He not only has a purpose, but only one purpose, for all history is but one. There are many scenes, but it is one drama; there are many pages, but it is one book; there are many leaves, but it is one tree, there are many provinces, and there be lords many and rulers many, yet there is but one empire, and God is the only Emperor.

O come let us worship and bow down before him: for the Lord is a great God, and a great King above all gods! (See Psalm 95:6 and Psalm 100:2-5.)

-C. H. SPURGEON

Peace with Humility

Let us run with endurance the race that is set before us,
fixing our eyes on Jesus, the author and perfecter of faith.
HEBREWS 12:1-2 NASB

Teresa of Avila warns us of the folly of paying attention to the small slights that others may or may not have offered us. Whether or not people insult us purposefully is not the point. We are quite capable of bearing up under insults and continuing down the path God plans for us. Keep your aim on God, and He won't let you be distracted and tripped up by your own pride.

God deliver us from people who wish to serve Him yet who are mindful of their own honor. Reflect how little they gain from this; for, as I have said, the very act of desiring honor robs us of it. You will say that these are little things which have to do with human nature and are not worth troubling about. But there is no small matter as extremely dangerous as are attention to honor and sensitivity to insult.

And how does this pride begin and grow? It may have its root, perhaps, in some trivial slight—hardly anything, in fact—and the devil will then induce someone else to consider it important. Then they will think it a kindness to tell you about it and to ask how you can allow yourself to be insulted so; and they will pray that God may give you patience and that you may offer it to Him, for even a saint could not bear more.

The devil is simply putting his deceitfulness into this other person's mouth; and, though you yourself were quite ready to bear the slight, you now are tempted in pride.

This human nature of ours is so wretchedly weak that, even while we are telling ourselves that there is nothing for us to make a fuss about, we imagine we are doing something virtuous, and begin to feel sorry for ourselves, particularly when we see that other people are sorry for us too.

-TERESA OF AVILA

"O Lord! All our trouble comes to us from not having our eyes fixed upon You. If we only looked at the path that we are walking, we should soon arrive; but we stumble and fall a thousand times and stray from the way because we do not set our eyes on You."

-TERESA OF AVILA

God's Purpose in Everything

Surely goodness and mercy shall follow me all the days of my life.
PSALM 23:6 NKJV

The writer of the encouraging best-seller *The Christian's Secret of a Happy Life*, Hannah Whitall Smith, didn't have an easy life, but a normal one with struggles and discouragements. However, she had inner peace and happiness because of her trust in God's goodness. She shares the following story of a woman who struggled with whether God really was in everything.

At last she began to ask God to teach her the truth about it, whether He really was in everything or not. After praying this for a few days, she had what she described as a vision. She thought she was in a perfectly dark place, and that there advanced toward her, from a distance, a body of light which gradually surrounded and enveloped her and everything around her. As it approached, a voice seemed to say, "This is the presence of God! This is the presence of God!"

While surrounded with this presence, all the great and awful things in life seemed to pass before her—fighting armies, wicked men, raging beasts, storms and pestilences, sin and suffering of every kind. She shrank back at first in terror; but she soon saw that the presence of God so surrounded and enveloped her that of each one of these things that not a lion could reach out its paw, nor a bullet fly through the air, except if the presence of God moved out of the way to permit it.

And she saw that if there were ever so thin a film, as it were, of this glorious Presence between herself and the most terrible violence, not a hair of her head could be ruffled, nor anything touch her, except when the Presence divided to let the evil through. Then all the small and annoying things of life passed before her; and equally she saw that there also she was so enveloped in this presence of God that not a cross look, nor a harsh word, nor a petty trial of any kind could affect her, unless God's encircling presence moved out of the way to let it.

Her difficulty vanished. Her question was answered forever. God was in everything; and to her from then on there were no second causes. She saw that her life came to her, day by day and hour by hour, directly from the hand of God.... And never again had she found any difficulty in abiding consent to His will and an unwavering trust in His care.

-Hannah Whitall Smith

As you go through this day, thank God for surrounding you with His protective presence and ask Him what you are to learn from those things that He allows in your life.

> *O Will, that wills good alone,*
> *You lead the way, You guide the best;*
> *A little child I follow on,*
> *And trusting lean upon Your breast.*
> -Hannah Whitall Smith

THE PURPOSE OF SUFFERING IS PATIENCE

Consider it a sheer gift, friends, when tests and challenges come at you from all sides. You know that under pressure, your faith-life is forced into the open and shows its true colors. So don't try to get out of anything prematurely. Let it do its work so you become mature and well-developed, not deficient in any way.

JAMES 1:2-4 MSG

Patience is something that grows slowly. For the Christian, patience is based on trust, faith, and humility. We trust that God is in control of our lives. We have faith that His purpose for us is good. And we are humble and willing to suffer in the present, knowing we will be blessed in the future.

Now, patience is usually cultivated by repeated instances of God answering prayer and blessing us when our problems seem too great. So we have problems, we feel overwhelmed, and we pray. We decide to hang in there, and then God answers our prayers either by fixing our problems or by giving us the strength and peace to make it through them—sometimes both. When God has answered your cry for help, your patience builds as your trust and faith in Him increase.

Whether your problems are great or small, try to bear them all patiently. The better you dispose yourself to suffer, the more wisely you act and the greater is the reward promised you. You will suffer more easily if your mind and habits are diligently trained to patience.

And it should not matter what type of suffering you will face.... No matter how great an adversity a patient person faces, no matter how often it comes or from whom it comes, they accept suffering gratefully from the hand of God, and count it a great gain.

For with God nothing that is suffered for His sake, no matter how small, can pass without reward. Be prepared for the fight, if you wish to gain the victory. Without struggle you cannot obtain the gift of patience, and if you refuse to suffer you are refusing the gift. But if you desire to be blessed, fight bravely and bear up patiently. Without labor there is no rest, and without fighting, no victory.

-THOMAS À KEMPIS, THE IMITATION OF CHRIST

"To be picked on and criticized by mean people is of little concern to a courageous person. But to be denounced and treated badly by good people, by our own friends and relatives, is a true test of virtue."

-FRANCES DE SALES

The Purpose in God's Truth

Anyone who believes in the Son of God has this testimony in his heart.
1 JOHN 5:10 NIV

We cannot have faith on our own. It comes from God. We don't naturally believe in the unseen and the unproved. Instead, God gives us faith as a gift. So when we need convincing of God's grace, love, or power, He will answer and strengthen our faith.

Because God knows us, He will make it exactly clear to us. He will even speak in our own words. John Bunyan often struggled with doubts. He had dark moments when he thought his sins were too great and his faith was too small. However, these moments were foundational to him and, he believed, foundational to every Christian. They built Bunyan's faith because when he doubted, God personally reassured and convinced him.

I sat under the ministry of holy Mr. Gifford. His doctrine, by God's grace, was much for my stability. This man made it much his business to deliver the people of God from all those hard and unsound tests that by nature we are prone to. He would bid us to take special heed that we didn't take any truth upon trust from any other people.

Instead, we were to cry mightily to God that He would convince us of the reality of the truth and set us down by His own Spirit in the holy word. "For," said he, "if you do otherwise, when temptation comes strongly upon you, because you have not received them with evidence from heaven, you will find you don't have the help and strength to resist."

—JOHN BUNYAN

> *Depth of mercy! Can there be*
> *mercy still reserved for me?*
> *Can my God his wrath forbear,*
> *me, the chief of sinners, spare?*
>
> *There for me the Savior stands,*
> *shows his wounds and spreads his hands.*
> *God is love! I know, I feel;*
> *Jesus weeps and loves me still.*
>
> —CHARLES WESLEY

Peace with a Pure Heart

I listen carefully to what God the Lord is saying,
for he speaks peace to his people.
PSALM 85:8 NLT

The founder of the Salvation Army, William Booth (1829-1912), had many trials in his life while serving God. Many of his fellow Christians disapproved of him because of his work with the poor. He went through much persecution by nonbelievers because of the Army's success at stopping alcoholism and consequently closing down lucrative taverns. In spite of these troubles, Booth had inner peace because of his pure heart directed at God.

You must not expect a life of uninterrupted gladness in this world. It cannot be. Our imperfect bodies, with all their pains and weaknesses; the temptations of the Devil, and the miseries of a world in rebellion against God, prevent anything like a life of unmixed rejoicing for you and me. But peace, "the peace of God, which surpasses all understanding," is your birthright, and with a Pure Heart, the treasure shall be yours (Philippians 4:7 NKJV).

I say again, that while you are here you must have certain strife. You cannot help it. You will have strife with the Devil. You will have strife with wicked men. They will fight you because you are for righteousness and God, and for the deliverance of men from their power.

But, Hallelujah! in the heart that is purified by the Holy Spirit, and sprinkled with the Blood of the Lamb, the strife with God has ceased, the war with conscience is ended, the fear of death and hell is over. The soul possessed of a Pure Heart has entered "the rest that remains to the people of God" (Hebrews 4:9 KJV).

Do you enjoy this rest, my friends? Is the inward strife over? Oh, make haste, and let the Blessed Spirit, who waits to sanctify you wholly, cast out the enemies of your soul! It is not your poverties, nor your persecutions, nor your afflictions, nor your ignorance, nor ever so many other things all put together, that prevent your perfect peace. Sin is the enemy; and when malice and indolence, and ambition and unbelief, and every other evil thing has been cast out, your peace shall flow as a river, and your righteousness shall abound as the waves of the sea. (See Isaiah 48:18.)

-WILLIAM BOOTH

"If we ever are to attain to true Divine Peace, and be completely united to God, all that is not absolutely necessary, either bodily or spiritually, must be cast off; everything that could interpose itself to an unlawful extent between us and Him, and lead us astray: for He alone will be Lord in our hearts, and none other; for Divine Love can admit of no rival."

-JOHANNES TAULER

Peace Comes from a Love Focused on God

You will keep him in perfect peace, whose mind is stayed on You,
because he trusts in You.
ISAIAH 26:3 NKJV

When our hearts rest on God, we can be at peace. The gentle theologian, Henry Scougal, points out that focusing our love on God gives us only love in return. God is strong and peaceful enough to take on all our troubles; and He doesn't have troubles in return to give us.

A lover is miserable, if the loved person is so. Two people, who have exchanged their hearts in love, have an interest in one another's happiness and misery. This combined interest makes love troublesome when it's placed on earth. The most fortunate person has enough grief to ruin the tranquility of their friend. It is hard to hold out when we are attacked on all sides, and suffer not only in our own life, but in another's.

But if God were the object of our love, we would share in an infinite happiness, without any mixture or possibility of diminution. We should rejoice to behold the glory of God, and receive comfort and pleasure from all the praises that men and angels do extol Him. It should delight us, beyond all expression, to consider, that the Beloved of our souls is infinitely happy in Himself. All His enemies cannot shake or unsettle

His throne for "Our God is in heaven; He does whatever He pleases" (Psalm 115:3 NKJV).

Behold, on what a sure foundation our happiness is built, when our soul is possessed with divine love, our will is transformed into the will of God, and our great desire is that our Maker should be pleased! O the peace, the rest, the satisfaction that attends such a frame of mind!

-HENRY SCOUGAL

> *I look up—into the face of Jesus,*
> *For there my heart can rest, my fears are stilled.*
> *And there is joy, and love, and light for darkness,*
> *And perfect peace, and every hope fulfilled.*
> -ANNIE JOHNSON FLINT

Peace from Impurity

How much more, then, will the blood of Christ, who through the eternal Spirit offered himself unblemished to God, cleanse our consciences from acts that lead to death, so that we may serve the living God!
HEBREWS 9:14 NIV

There comes a point in each person's life when they realize their own sinful nature and their inability to be good simply by trying harder. Sure, everyone can do a little better if they try, but the heart doesn't change for the better unless it encounters God. William Booth tells of the point where the soul turns to God and asks to be cleansed.

The soul, tired of conflict, hating its internal evils, weeping over the pride and malice, and envy and selfishness that it still finds within, rises up, and cries out:

"Tell me what to do to be pure,
In the sight of the All-seeing eyes.
Tell me, is there no thorough cure,
No escape from the sins I despise?
Tell me, can I never be free
From this terrible bondage within?
Is there no deliverance for me?
Must I always have sin dwell within?"

To this question God sends the glad answer back: "Then I will sprinkle clean water on you, and you shall be clean; I will cleanse you from all your filthiness and from all your idols. I will give you a new heart and put a new spirit within you; I will take the heart of stone out of your flesh and give you a heart of flesh. I will put My Spirit within you and cause you to walk in My statutes, and you will keep My judgments and do them" (Ezekiel 36:25-27 NKJV). "Everything is possible for him who believes" (Mark 9:23 NIV). Then the soul believes, the sanctifying Spirit falls, and there is Salvation from all sin.

-WILLIAM BOOTH

*Everyone who has this hope in Him purifies himself,
just as He is pure.*
1 JOHN 3:3 NKJV

Peace with God's Limitless Love

Do not be anxious about anything, but in everything,
by prayer and petition, with thanksgiving,
present your requests to God.
PHILIPPIANS 4:6 NIV

Just as a crying baby immediately starts to smile when its mother enters the room, so we, too, calm down and rest when we sense the presence of God. When we are worried or fearful or doubtful, the only answer is to look to God.

When we consider His amazing nature, full of love, power, wisdom, control, and gentleness, we are more able to stop worrying about our problems because in comparison to God they are smaller and easier to manage. The following poem by Annie Johnson Flint (1866-1932) is one to slowly read and meditate over. Saying it aloud will encourage the heart and strengthen the soul.

"God gives more grace when the burdens grow greater.
He sends more strength when the labors increase,
To added affliction He addeth His mercy,
To multiplied trials, His multiplied peace.
When we have exhausted our store of endurance,
When our strength has failed 'ere the day is half done;
When we reach the end of our hoarded resources
Our Father's full giving is only begun.

His love has no limit, His grace has no measure.
His power no boundary known unto men;
For out of His infinite riches in Jesus
He giveth and giveth and giveth again."

-ANNIE JOHNSON FLINT

The Way to a Pure Heart

[Jesus said,] "Blessed are the pure in heart, for they shall see God."
MATTHEW 5:8 NASB

A pure heart, or a life in the center of God's will, is not impossible. It is not an idealistic dream, but a reality for Christian living. William Booth gives a practical understanding of a pure heart and how it can lead to a life full of faith, peace, hope, and love.

First, a Pure Heart is not a heart that is never tempted. Possibly there is no such thing in this world, nor ever has been, as a non-tempted heart, that is, a man or a woman who has never been exposed to temptation to commit sin. Not only was our Blessed Lord tempted by the Devil in the wilderness, but He was beset with evil attractions all the way through His life. St. Paul expressly tells us that our Savior was in all points tempted like as we are, but He effectually resisted the world, the flesh, and the Devil, and came through the trying ordeal without a stain.

Second, a Pure Heart is not a heart that cannot suffer. Beyond question, Jesus Christ had a Pure Heart. He was Holy and undefiled, and yet He was "The Man of Sorrows."

Third, a Pure Heart is not a heart that cannot sin. Adam was pure when he came from the hands of his Maker. God pronounced him to be good. But, led away by Satan, he lost his purity, and was cast out of Eden into a world of sin and sorrow and death.

Finally, a Pure Heart does not mean any experience of Purity, however blessed it may be, cannot increase in enjoyment, usefulness, and power. Pull the weeds out of your garden, and the flowers ... will grow faster, flourish more abundantly, and become more fruitful.

Just so, this very moment, let Jesus Christ purge the garden of your souls of envy and pride, and remove the poisonous plants of malice and selfishness and every other evil thing. Then faith and peace, and hope and love, and humility and courage, and all the other beautiful flowers of Paradise will flourish in more charming beauty and more abundant fruitfulness.

What, then, is a Pure Heart? A Pure Heart is a heart that has been cleansed by the Holy Spirit from all sin, and enabled to please God in all it does; to love Him with all its powers, and its neighbor as itself.

-WILLIAM BOOTH

> *Grant us, dear Lord, from evil ways*
> *True absolution and release:*
> *And bless us, more than in past days,*
> *With purity and inward peace.*
> -FREDERICK W. FABER

The Purpose of Prayer Is Purity

*Be joyful in hope, patient in affliction,
faithful in prayer.*
ROMANS 12:12 NIV

Although many believe in the power and miracles of prayer, very few actually spend large amounts of time in prayer. The fourteenth-century Christian, Walter Hilton, explains that prayer is necessary and helpful because it is the only way to grace and purity.

Prayer is profitable and speedy to be used for the getting of purity of heart by destroying of sin and bringing in virtues. Not that prayer is for you to make our Lord know what you desire, because He knows well enough what you need. But prayer is to dispose you and make you ready and able, as a clean vessel, to receive the grace that our Lord would freely give you.

This grace cannot be felt until you are purified by the fire of desire in devout prayer. For though prayer is not what causes our Lord to give us grace, it is the way or means by which grace freely given comes into a soul.

-WALTER HILTON

Through prayer we find God, become more like Him, and receive His grace. Don't be discouraged when prayer is hard and your mind wanders. Instead confess your difficulty and ask God to increase your desire to pray.

"When you feel yourself most indisposed to prayer do not yield to it, but strive and endeavor to pray even when you think you cannot pray."

-ARTHUR HILDERSAM

Longing for Peace

"The Lord make His face shine upon you, and be gracious to you; The Lord lift up His countenance upon you, and give you peace."
NUMBERS 6:25-26 NKJV

The only peace that satisfies is the peace of Christ. God is working in the lives of those who are far from Him. He prepares their hearts with a longing for peace. George Müller (1805-1898) writes in his autobiography about his first encounter with God and the obvious peace he felt spending time in a Christian house.

On Saturday afternoon, about the middle of November 1925, I had taken a walk with my friend Beta. On our return he said to me that he was in the habit of going on Saturday evenings to the house of a Christian, where there was a meeting. He told me that they read the Bible, sang, prayed, and read a printed sermon. No sooner had I heard this than it was to me as if I had found something after which I had been seeking all my life long. We went together in the evening. As I did not know the manners of believers, and the joy they have in seeing poor sinners . . . I made an apology for coming. The kind answer of the dear brother I shall never forget. He said, "Come as often as you please; house and heart are open to you."

We sat down and sang a hymn. Then Brother Kayser, now a missionary in Africa, fell on his knees and asked a blessing on our meeting. This kneeling down made a deep impression upon me; for I had never either seen any one on his knees, nor had I ever myself prayed on my knees. He then read a chapter and a printed sermon. At the close we sang another hymn, and then the master of the house prayed. While he prayed, my feeling was something like this: "I could not pray as well, though I am much more learned than this illiterate man." The whole made a deep impression on me. I was happy; though, if I had been asked why I was happy, I could not have clearly explained it.

When we walked home, I said to Beta, "All we have seen on our journey to Switzerland, and all our former pleasures, are as nothing in comparison with this evening." Whether I fell on my knees when I returned home, I do not remember; but this I know, that I lay peaceful and happy in my bed.

- GEORGE MÜLLER

As Christians, the peace of God flows through our lives. Ask the Lord to make you aware of everyone you meet and their need for His peace.

The Purpose of Living

Whatever you do, do all to the glory of God.
1 CORINTHIANS 10:31 NASB

Oftentimes we get distracted and discouraged by the busyness of life. We find ourselves going through the motions of our routine without seeing the big picture. Frances de Sales (1567-1622) reminds us that God created us for a purpose; and that purpose is to know Him in an ongoing relationship and to reflect His love and light by seeking Him more.

God did not bring you into the world because He had any need of you, useless as you are; but so that He might show His goodness through you, giving you His grace for His glory. Therefore, He gave you a mind that you might know Him, memory that you might do His deeds, a will that you might choose to love Him, imagination that you might begin to grasp His mercies, sight that you might look at the marvels of His works, and speech that you might praise Him. . . .

Being created and placed in the world for this intent, all contrary actions should be rejected, and you should also avoid anything that does not encourage it. Consider how unhappy they are . . . who live as though they were created only to build and plant, to heap up riches and amuse themselves with trifles.

Humble yourself because you have rarely considered your purpose. Abhor your past life. Turn to God. Thank God, who has made you for so gracious a purpose.

Only You, my God and Savior, shall be the object of my thoughts. No more will I give my mind to ideas that are displeasing to You. All the days of my life I will dwell upon the greatness of Your Goodness, so lovingly poured out upon me. From now on You shall be the delight of my heart, the resting-place of all my affections.... You have made me, O Lord, for Yourself, that I may eternally enjoy the immensity of Your Glory. When shall I be worthy of You, when shall I know how to bless You as I should?

-FRANCIS DE SALES

We have been made to glorify the Lord in all we do. Like a lover, we will respond and reflect the love of our Beloved.

The Purpose of Love

Mostly what God does is love you. Keep company with him and learn a life of love. Observe how Christ loved us. His love was not cautious but extravagant. He didn't love in order to get something from us but to give everything of himself to us. Love like that.
EPHESIANS 5:2 MSG

The purpose of love is to change the one giving it and the one receiving it. A person with love looks only to do the best for the object of their love. Henry Scougal (1650-1678) writes that God is our true love and we are His.

We see how easily couples or friends slide into the imitation of the one they adore; and how, even before they are aware, they begin to resemble them, not only in their actions, but also in their voice and gesture, and their expression or manner. Certainly we should also copy the virtues and inward beauties of the soul, if they were the true object and motive of our love. But because all people we encounter have their mixture of good and bad, we are always in danger to be corrupted by placing our affections on them.

The true way to improve and ennoble our souls is by fixing our love on the divine perfection of God, that we may have them always before us, and derive an impression of them on ourselves; and "beholding as in a mirror the glory of the Lord, are being transformed into the same image from glory to glory, just as by the Spirit of the Lord" (2 Corinthians 3:18 NKJV). Those who, with a generous and holy ambition, have raised their eyes towards that uncreated beauty and goodness, and fixed their affection there, are of quite another spirit and of a more excellent and heroic temper, than the rest of the world. They cannot help but infinitely dislike all unworthy things and will not entertain any low or base thoughts that might disparage their high and noble purpose.

Love is the greatest and most excellent thing we are masters of and therefore it is folly and baseness to give it unworthily. It is indeed the only thing we can call our own: other things may be taken from us by violence, but none can ravish our love. If any thing else be counted ours by giving our love, we give all, so far as we make over our hearts and wills, by which we possess our other enjoyments. It is not possible to refuse Him anything, to whom by love we have given ourselves. . . . Certainly love is the worthiest present we can offer unto God.

—HENRY SCOUGAL

Thank You, Lord, for giving us Your love in the form of Your Son and Spirit. May our hearts change as we turn our love more and more to You.

God's Purposes Are for Our Good

We know that God causes all things to work together for good to those who love God, to those who are called according to His purpose.
ROMANS 8:28 NASB

When we are facing great troubles or experiencing pain, it is difficult not to drift into deep despair. We find it hard to believe that God's plans and purposes are really for our benefit. We worry that maybe God doesn't care about us or about our suffering—that even if His plans are good, they may not be for our personal good.

But these discouraging thoughts are lies. God does have the ability to orchestrate the happenings and occurrences of all people for their good. When we turn to God, give our worries and our troubles over to Him and stop struggling against Him in fear, He can and will bless us. The answer, says Alphonsus di Ligouri, is to seek God, and all will be well.

He is always ready to use any occurrence in our life to shape and change us to be more like Him.

"Little man," says Saint Augustine, "grow up. What are you seeking in your search for happiness? Seek the one good that embraces all others." Whom do you seek, friend, if you seek not God? Seek Him, find Him, cleave to Him; bind your will to His with bands of steel and you will live always at peace in this life and in the next.

God wills only our good; God loves us more than anybody else can or does love us. His will is that no one should lose their soul, that everyone should save and sanctify their soul: "Not willing that any should perish but that all should come to repentance" (2 Peter 3:9 NKJV). "This is the will of God, your sanctification" (1 Thessalonians 4:3 NKJV). God has made the attainment of our happiness, His glory.

-ALPHONSUS DI LIGOURI

God, we're sorry that we fear Your will when we should be looking forward to it. Remind us again that You love to bless us in all circumstances.

> "His will be done,"
> We say with sighs and trembling,
> Expecting trial, bitter loss and tears.
> And then how doth He answer us?
> With blessings,
> And sweet rebuking of our faithless fears.
>
> -ANNIE JOHNSON FLINT

God's Ways with Backsliders

"My people have committed two sins: They have forsaken me, the spring of living water, and have dug their own cisterns, broken cisterns that cannot hold water."

JEREMIAH 2:13 NIV

Sometimes the hardest people to talk to about God are those who once knew Him well but have since turned away. We still love our friends who have turned their backs on God, but we don't know how to encourage them. If we lecture them, they can distance themselves from us as well as God. But if we ignore their changed heart, we risk pretending that nothing is wrong and supporting their bad choices. The outspoken preacher Dwight L. Moody focuses on how God looks at His people who turn from Him.

The most tender and loving words to be found in the whole of the Bible are from Jehovah to those who have left Him without a cause. Hear how He argues with them: "Your own wickedness will correct you, and your backslidings will rebuke you. Know therefore and see that it is an evil and bitter thing that you have forsaken the Lord your God, and the fear of Me is not in you" (Jeremiah 2:19 NKJV).

I do not exaggerate when I say that I have seen hundreds of backsliders come back; and I have asked them if they have not found it an evil and a bitter thing to leave the Lord. You cannot find a real backslider, who has known the Lord, that won't admit that it is an evil and a bitter thing to turn away from Him. I do not know of any one verse more used to bring back wanderers than that very one. May it bring you back if you have wandered into the far country.

-D. L. MOODY

God, just as we have wandered and turned back only to discover Your overwhelming love and forgiveness, we lift up our friends and family that once called You Lord.

> *O that I could repent!*
> *Thou, by Thy two-edged sword,*
> *My soul and spirit part,*
> *Strike with the hammer of Thy Word,*
> *And break my stubborn heart!*
>
> -CHARLES WESLEY

Determining God's Purpose in the Little and Big Things

[Jesus said,] "God will always give what is right to his people who cry to him night and day, and he will not be slow to answer them."
LUKE 18:7-8 NCV

God cares about our lives. He cares about what is important to us, because He genuinely loves us. So when we have decisions to make, He is ready and willing to guide us. Frances de Sales' advice for those seeking God's will is profound and practical. He warns us against seeking God's will in all the little decisions of daily life and in then being distracted and getting nothing done. He instead exclaims the need to seek God's will in the big stuff.

I am to warn you of a troublesome temptation which often crosses the way of such souls as have a great desire to do what is most according to God's will. The enemy at every turn puts them in doubt whether it is God's will for them to do one thing rather than another. For example, whether they should eat with a friend or not, whether they should wear grey or black clothes, whether they should fast Friday or Saturday. And while they are busy and anxious to find out what is the better choice, they let time slip when they could have done many good things for God's glory.

Some things should be considered carefully. The choice of one's vocation, the plan of some business of great importance, of some work occupying much time, of some very great expense, the change of residence, the choice of friends, and the like, deserve to be seriously pondered, in order to see what is most according to the will of God.

And even in matters of importance we are to use a great humility, and not to think we can find out God's will by force of thought and subtlety of debate. Instead, we must ask for the light of the Holy Ghost, make our focus the seeking of His good pleasure, take the advice of our spiritual mentor, and, perhaps, of two or three other spiritual persons. Then we must resolve and determine what to do in the name of God. Afterwards we must not question the decision, but devoutly, peacefully, and firmly keep and pursue it.

And although the difficulties, temptations and the different circumstances which occur in the course of acting out our decision might cause us some doubt as to whether we had made a good choice, we must still remain secure, and not regard all this. Consider that if we had made another choice, it may have been a hundred times worse. Once the holy decision is made, we are never to doubt of the holiness of acting it out; for unless we fail it cannot fail.

-Frances de Sales

God cares more about our character than about our career. If we seek Him regularly in prayer, are wise in making big decisions, and keep a listening ear and an open heart, He won't let us go down the wrong path.

"God's purpose for you is to be His servant"

-OSWALD CHAMBERS

Peace and Blessings in Suffering

We love because he first loved us.
1 JOHN 4:19 NIV

The fact that God allows suffering, trials, and persecution can be a hard thing to grasp, especially in light of His eternal love for us. But we must remember that He does love us, and He will bless us at every turn. All we have to do is to humbly seek His will. The following two Christian poets and hymn writers, Annie Johnson Flint and Fanny Crosby, both suffered, yet they never doubted God's innate goodness as He blessed them throughout their lives.

A few years after high school, Annie Johnson Flint's adoptive parents died, and she developed arthritis that left her bedridden for the rest of her life. She was dependent on others for money and care, but remained optimistic. She knew that God would give her grace and peace sufficient for each day. She continued writing poetry and encouraging others by declaring the goodness of God. Flint's following poem tells of life's suffering and the goodness God promises.

> *God has not promised skies always blue,*
> *Flower strewn pathways all our lives through;*
> *God has not promised sun without rain,*
> *Joy without sorrow, peace without pain.*

> *But God has promised strength for the day,*
> *Rest for the labor, light for the way,*
> *Grace for the trials, help from above,*
> *Unfailing sympathy, undying love.*

The hymn writer Fanny Crosby (1820-1915) would have denied that she ever suffered. Her blindness wasn't a hardship, or even a disability; instead, it was a blessing from God. She told others that she wished she had always been blind, "Because when I get to heaven, the first face that would ever gladden my sight will be that of my Savior." At age eight, Fanny wrote a poem declaring the blessings she enjoyed. She went on to write more than 9,000 hymns, including *Blessed Assurance* and *Safe in the Arms of Jesus*. The following is the first poem she wrote as a child, declaring her joy to be alive.

> *Oh, what a happy soul I am,*
> *Although I cannot see!*
> *I am resolved that in this world*
> *Contented I will be.*
>
> *How many blessings I enjoy,*
> *That other people don't,*
> *To weep and sigh because I'm blind*
> *I cannot, and I won't!*

Fanny Crosby's joy of life wasn't an illusion. It was a true reality of the blessings of Jesus. Both Crosby and Flint knew that no matter what problems or experiences we may go through in life, God can and will use them to bless us and to bless others.

Don't be discouraged when things aren't going the way you planned. God has a greater plan, one you cannot imagine!

> *"I will bless you; I will make your name great, and you will be a blessing."*
> GENESIS 12:2 NIV

The Peace of Healing

"I, the Lord, am your healer."
Exodus 15:26 NASB

God is the great healer. Jesus never turned down anyone who asked to be healed. God loves to heal and wants us to ask Him for healing.

However, the Christian counselor, Keith Martin, said there are two possible responses when we pray for healing. The first response is healing. Sometimes this healing first involves repenting of sins, and other times it involves believing and focusing on God's truth and love.

The second response God can give is not as clear. When we pray for healing and the sick person is not healed, we can expect God to then give them peace. We should pray and wait until they receive the peace that transcends understanding. God will overcome any pain or inconvenience they experience with the blessing of His presence. This healing of peace is greater than the physical hurt.

There are many whom God heals and there are many whom He doesn't. And there are those whom He tells to wait for His perfect timing.

God will never impose suffering or allow suffering without blessing us. It is part of His good nature to bless and care for us. He is the Good Shepherd, and He cares for His sheep.

The Purpose of Servant Leaders

"Love the Lord your God with all your passion and prayer and muscle and intelligence—and ... love your neighbor as well as you do yourself."
Luke 10:27 MSG

The purpose of servant leadership is to first serve God and second to serve people. Or to love God and love people. This is what Christ did on earth. He spent time with God in prayer and then taught and healed those who came across His path and asked for help. He never viewed an interruption as such, but instead he saw each as an opportunity to love and do God's will.

To serve God means to obey His commands. But to first obey, we must know His commands and understand them. Therefore, we read His Word and spend time in prayer asking for clarification. These three things—obedience, reading the Bible, and prayer—all encompass what serving God really is: Enjoying Him and glorifying His name.

To serve people involves two things—helping people's physical and spiritual needs. If people are physically starving, they won't be able to focus or understand the necessity of spiritual food until we have given them actual food. So our service is like Christ's; we help those we encounter, and we bless them as we do.

Sometimes serving is as easy as offering someone a ride, helping fix a car, babysitting, or taking someone out for lunch and being a compassionate listener. Be aware of whom God places in your path and be open to changing your plans to help others.

A Fixed Purpose to Know God

Listen, O my people, to my instruction; incline your ears to the words of my mouth.
PSALM 78:1 NASB

The Reverend Osborn Dickerson, a former slave in New Orleans, refused to stop seeking and praising and telling others about Christ. He had a fixed purpose to know God. The following story by Joanna P. Moore shows how his purpose did not change in spite of opposition.

Once, near dark, I was sitting away back in my cabin, so interested in reading about the blessed Savior that I did not hear the master till he stood right over me. "Osborn," he said, "do you know how to read?" "Yes," I answered all in a tremble. "Did you know it's against my rules?" "Yes, I did." He then snatched the book, tore and threw it in the fire. That was like taking the very heart out of me. I expected the hundred lashes, but I prayed and the master walked out of the cabin without another word. I said, "That is God who shut the lions' mouths; He is the same God today."

I had been preaching to the slaves about Jesus and singing the hymns that I could remember. Several became Christians and one of them was Stephen, the servant who waited on the master. He had been with him many years, and had nursed him when he was a child.

About a year after the loss of my Bible this servant got sick and died. The master was mighty sorry. As he sat by the bedside when he was dying, Stephen said, "Master, I have one request to make; will you grant it?"

"Yes, Stephen, anything you want I would do."

"Well, after I am dead, please master, let Osborn bury me. Let him sing and pray at my grave."

This the master promised. The cart came and carried the coffin to the servants' graveyard. The master was there on horseback, the other friends standing around the grave. I prayed and repeated some verses about the resurrection and sang, lining out the hymn.

When I came to the words in the song, "The tall, the wise, the reverent head must be as low as ours," the master uttered a cry and fell from his horse. The servants carried him away. The next morning he sent for me. Now again I prayed to Daniel's God, for I feared master would stop my preaching. "Osborn," he said, "you may teach your religion here on my place as much as you like and as you have time to preach, but do not go onto any other plantation, for it is against the law."

That is the way the Lord opened the Red Sea for me. I never got another Bible until the Yankees came. The first thing I said to them was, "Give me a Bible"; and I got one. That was as great a joy to me as my freedom.

-OSBORN DICKERSON, AS TOLD TO JOANNA P. MOORE

As Osborn Dickerson continued to seek God, God blessed him and answered his prayers in a miraculous way. As we seek God, so He, too, will bless us.

The Purpose of Shepherding

[Jesus said,] "I am the good shepherd; I know my sheep and my sheep know me—just as the Father knows me and I know the Father— and I lay down my life for the sheep."
JOHN 10:14-15 NIV

There are some people who are born leaders. They walk and others follow. Other people don't have the natural ability but still find themselves in positions of leadership. They must take the time to learn what is necessary for successful leadership. Beyond the tools necessary to make people listen and follow, leaders must know what their purpose for leadership is. Are they in the world to make changes, to gain power, or to serve God and help others?

Christ is the center of servant leadership. He first served His Father, and then He served the people. He says He is the good shepherd. What does a shepherd do? A shepherd takes care of the sheep.

In Ezekiel 34, there is a list of duties of a shepherd. A good shepherd takes care of the flock, strengthens the weak, heals the sick, binds up the injured, brings back the strays, and searches for the lost. This is love. A good shepherd is full of love for the sheep.

As leaders, this love is our top priority.

The purpose of leadership is to take care of the weak. Christ said that it is not the healthy who need a doctor, but the sick. Our duty is to the sick, the weak, the poor, the orphans, and the widows. The majority of the time, this is to be taken literally. However, the poor and weak in spirit also need to be taken care of. Those who are physically poor are often also spiritually poor and are aware of their poverty. But those who are physically rich and healthy usually aren't aware of their spiritual poverty.

Pray for God to show you the needs of His people. They may be physically or spiritually needy, or both. Then ask for guidance in how you can best serve them. Sometimes all God wants is your prayers, and He will change hearts and lives. Other times He will work directly through you as you interact with His love.

> *"They will know that I, the Lord their God, am with them and that they, the house of Israel, are my people," declares the Sovereign Lord. "You my sheep, the sheep of my pasture, are people, and I am your God," declares the Sovereign Lord.*
>
> EZEKIEL 34:30-31 NIV

Our Purpose Is to Worship God

All the nations you have made will come and worship before you,
O Lord; they will bring glory to your name.
PSALM 86:9 NIV

God's ultimate purpose for us is to worship Him. In Genesis 12:2-3 NIV, when God made a covenant with Abraham, He told him that "all peoples on earth will be blessed through you." This is part one of God's purpose for mankind—that all will be blessed because of God's goodness. A common reminder in the Old Testament is "the Lord is gracious and compassionate." His good and compassionate nature overflows us with blessings. Our natural response is to worship and thank Him.

Part two of God's purpose for mankind is for this blessing to result in all peoples willingly bowing down and glorifying the name of the Lord. Not only does this please God, but it also fulfills His purpose for us. We align with His will and do what we do best—praise His name and declare His goodness.

"Did God create you for His glory or for your joy? He created you so that you might spend eternity glorifying Him by enjoying Him forever. In other words, you do not have to choose between glorifying God and enjoying God."

-JOHN PIPER

The following song by Millicent D. Kingham (1866-1927) reassures us as Christians that God's purpose will be accomplished and that it is being accomplished right now.

> *God is working his purpose out,*
> *As year succeeds to year:*
> *God is working his purpose out,*
> *And the time is drawing near;*
> *Nearer and nearer draws the time,*
> *The time that shall surely be,*
> *When the earth shall be filled with the glory of God*
> *As the waters cover the sea.*
>
> -MILLICENT D. KINGHAM

When we worship God in church or alone, we are preparing our hearts for the day we long for when "the earth shall be filled with the knowledge of the glory of the Lord, as the waters cover the sea" (Habakkuk 2:14 KJV).

The Purpose of Life

[Jesus said,] "If anyone is willing to do His will, he will know of the teaching, whether it is of God or whether I speak from Myself."
JOHN 7:17 NASB

There is something special about the life that a Christian leads, following and learning from the Holy Spirit. God's lessons are above any we could comprehend or come up with on our own. God's truth is often beyond mere human understanding. He gives us explanations of it in the Scripture, but to truly understand, we have to follow and learn from Him in "real life."

God gives us our lives for a purpose. He uses each and every experience to change us and teach us about Him and about ourselves. These lessons are more real than the ones in books. They are significant and true. We understand them in the core of our being. Lessons we've been taught are important, but they are only explanations or outlines of the lessons God teaches us through life experiences. The following paragraph, written by Evelyn Underhill (1875-1941), emphasizes the necessity of real-life practice of Christian virtues and truths.

"Books," said Saint Augustine, after his conversion, "could not teach me charity." We still keep on thinking they can. We do not realize . . . the utter distinctness of God and the things of God. Psychology of religion cannot teach us prayer, and ethics cannot teach us love. Only Christ can do that, and He teaches by the direct method, in and among the circumstances of life. He does not mind about our being comfortable. He wants us to be strong, able to tackle life and be Christians, be apostles in life, so we must be trained by the ups and downs, the rough-and-tumble of life. Team games are compulsory in the school of Divine Love—there is no getting into a corner with a nice, spiritual book.

-EVELYN UNDERHILL

Don't be afraid to periodically ask God in prayer, "What are You teaching me?" and listen for His response. God is always speaking and teaching us, even when He is silent. The biggest lesson that God repeatedly teaches us is "I love you" and "You are loveable."

"The Kingdom disciple teaches from his or her storehouse of personal experiences of God's rule in the commonplace events of real life."

-DALLAS WILLARD

The Purpose of the Holy Spirit is Power

[Jesus said,] *"You will receive power when the Holy Spirit has come upon you; and you shall be My witnesses both in Jerusalem, and in all Judea and Samaria, and even to the remotest part of the earth."*

ACTS 1:8 NASB

Many Christians debate as to whether the Holy Spirit indwells us from the moment we ask Christ to be our Lord or later. This debate cannot be easily resolved. However, the ongoing argument clouds the true purpose and need of the Holy Spirit in our lives.

The Holy Spirit brings power—supernatural power that changes lives. The following story of Dwight L. Moody shows how amazing it is when we live our lives with the Holy Spirit's power.

In his early days D. L. Moody was a great hustler; he had a tremendous desire to do something, but he had no real power. He worked very largely in his own strength.

But there were two humble Free Methodist women who used to come over to his meetings in the Y.M.C.A. These two women would come to Mr. Moody at the close of his meetings and say: "We are praying for you." Finally, Mr. Moody became somewhat nettled and said to them one night, "Why are you praying for me? Why don't you pray for the unsaved?"

They replied: "We are praying that you may get the power." Mr. Moody did not know what that meant, but he got to thinking about it, and then went to these women and said: "I wish you would tell me what you mean." They told him about the definite baptism with the Holy Spirit. Then he asked that he might pray with them and not they merely pray for him.

Not long after, one day on his way to England, he was walking up Wall Street in New York; . . . and in the midst of the bustle and hurry of that city his prayer was answered. The power of God fell upon him as he walked up the street, and he had to hurry off to the house of a friend and ask that he might have a room by himself. In that room he stayed alone for hours; and the Holy Spirit came upon him, filling his soul with such joy that at last he had to ask God to withhold His hand, in case he die on the spot from joy.

He went out from that place with the power of the Holy Spirit upon him, and when he got to London . . . the power of God worked through him mightily.

-R. A. TORREY

If you feel powerless and unable to change lives for Christ, pray for the touch of the Holy Spirit. Your life will never be the same.

The Purpose of Continuing Prayer

> [Jesus said,] "Ask and it will be given to you; seek and you will find; knock and the door will be opened to you. For everyone who asks receives; he who seeks finds; and to him who knocks, the door will be opened."
>
> MATTHEW 7:7-8 NIV

It is easy to pray when we see an immediate positive response. However, the hard part about prayer is that often we see no response, and we have to trust that God is indeed listening. We have to keep praying even when we see nothing happen. Patient determination is often the only successful method of intercessory prayer. Dwight L. Moody writes of the importance of continuing prayer with an example of a wife praying for her non-Christian husband.

I heard of a wife in England who had an unconverted husband. She resolved that she would pray every day for twelve months for his conversion. Every day at twelve o'clock she went to her room alone and cried to God. Her husband would not allow her to speak to him on the subject; but she could speak to God on his behalf.

It may be that you have a friend who does not wish to be spoken with about their salvation; you can do as this woman did—go and pray to God about it. The twelve months passed away, and there was no sign of his yielding. She resolved to pray for six months longer; so every day she went alone and prayed for the conversion of her husband.

The six months passed, and still there was no sign, no answer. The question arose in her mind, could she give him up? "No," she said, "I will pray for him as long as God gives me breath." That very day, when he came home to dinner, instead of going into the dining room he went upstairs. She waited, and waited, and waited; but he did not come down to dinner.

Finally she went to his room, and found him on his knees crying to God to have mercy upon him. God convicted him of sin. He not only became a Christian, but the Word of God had free course, and was glorified in him. God then used him mightily. That was God answering the prayers of this Christian wife; she knocked, and knocked, till the answer came.

-D. L. Moody

Don't get discouraged when you are praying for a loved one to turn to Christ. God loves them more than you do. He desires that all would become His children. Keep praying for them; you are praying for God's will to be done on earth.

"Knock away till sundown; and then come again, and knock all tomorrow."

-D. L. Moody

The Purpose of Dreams

"There is hope for your future," declares the Lord.
JEREMIAH 31:17 NIV

When we are considering our future hopes and plans, we should first remember that our main purpose is to glorify God with our lives, with our character, and with our actions. God enjoys us most when we spend time with Him and enjoy His presence. He is more interested in our character than our career. However, most of us still want to have fulfilling careers that we enjoy and that give us a sense of purpose.

Discovering God's secondary purposes for your life can be difficult. For Christians, living is a process in which we seek God and learn from Him. There often isn't one specific purpose for our lives. Very few of us have a strong sense of a calling, like Billy Graham to preach or Mother Teresa to nurse the poor and dying. We instead have strengths and likes that lead us. And often there are different periods of our lives when we focus on different things like school, family, and retirement. What can be difficult is wanting to seek God's will in your life and your career, but being unsure of how to take the next step to make it happen.

If we are to glorify the Lord in what we do, it helps to be doing something we're suited to and enjoy. Psalm 37:4 NIV says, "Delight yourself in the Lord; and he will give you the desires of your heart." This promise is twofold. Not only can

God answer and give you what you desire, but He can also place these desires in your heart in the first place. If you spend time regularly in the Lord's presence, He will speak to you and teach you, and He will also gradually change the scope and direction of your dreams. Then, when you are seeking and heading to work in the direction of your dreams, you will be following in the footsteps of the Lord.

We shouldn't be afraid to dream and let our dreams guide our future plans. God is an imaginative and loving God who encourages dreaming. However, when we dream, we should hold loosely to our hopes and desires, giving them over to the Lord. There's always a chance that He has even bigger plans and a brighter future than you can imagine. Often the dreams that He plants in our heart are only glimpses or outlines of possibilities that we couldn't understand or imagine. He gives them to us so that we can get excited with Him, and we can continue spending time and turning our plans over to Him so that the beautiful things He sees in the future can come into existence for us.

Ask God what your dreams are. Keep a pencil in your hand and jot down ideas and verses.

The Peace of Unity in Prayer

Very early in the morning, while it was still dark, Jesus got up, left the house and went off to a solitary place, where he prayed.
MARK 1:35 NIV

Prayer is intimate communication with God. It is more than just words, and it can be without words. Prayer is sometimes asking, sometimes telling. It is the communication in an ongoing relationship between people and God. The young theologian, Henry Scougal, reminds us that Christ had a constant unity with God in prayer that we can share.

One instance of Christ's love to God was His delight in conversing with Him by prayer, which made Him frequently retire himself from the world, and, with the greatest devotion and pleasure, spend whole nights in that heavenly exercise, though He had not sins to confess, and few secular interests to pray for. But, we may say His whole life was a kind of prayer; a constant course of communion with God.

-HENRY SCOUGAL

We long to be like Christ and echo the words of Keith Green, "Make my life a prayer to You." The following song by the preacher and gospel hymn writer Charles Albert Tindley

(1851-1933) offers up the goal of personal unity with Christ.

> *Nothing between my soul and my Savior,*
> *Naught of this world's delusive dream;*
> *I have renounced all sinful pleasure;*
> *Jesus is mine, there's nothing between.*
>
> *Nothing between, like worldly pleasure;*
> *Habits of life, though harmless they seem;*
> *Must not my heart from Him ever sever;*
> *He is my all, there's nothing between.*
>
> *Nothing between, e'en many hard trials,*
> *Though the whole world against me convene;*
> *Watching with prayer and much self denial,*
> *I'll triumph at last, there's nothing between.*

-CHARLES ALBERT TINDLEY

Unity with God in Christ is available to us. We can seek and receive His love and presence each time we turn our eyes and minds to Him in prayer.

The Purpose of Moses

No prophet has risen in Israel like Moses,
whom the Lord knew face to face.
DEUTERONOMY 34:10 NIV

God's purpose for Moses was to show His power and glory to the Egyptians and to the surrounding peoples. And the best way to do this was through a humble vessel. The importance of Moses is not his willingness, nor his amazing abilities, but instead it seems to be his lack of abilities. Sure, Moses started out as a statesman and an orator, but he made severe mistakes and learned the wisdom of patience in the desert. Matthew Henry's (1662-1714) commentary on Exodus contains the following excerpts that are an example and an encouragement for Christians seeking to work for God like the prophet Moses.

The first appearance of God to Moses found him tending sheep. This seems a poor employment for a man of his talents and background, yet he rests satisfied with it; and learned meekness and contentment—for which he is more noted in the Scriptures, than for all his learning.

Formerly Moses thought himself able to deliver Israel, and set himself to the work too hastily. Now, when he is the fittest person on earth for it, he knows his own weakness. This was the effect of more knowledge of God and of himself. Formerly, self-confidence mingled with strong faith and great zeal, now sinful distrust of God crept in under the garb of humility. But all his objections are answered by God with, "Certainly I will be with you. That is enough."

Moses continued going backward to the work God designed for him because there was much cowardice, laziness, and unbelief in him. We must not judge people by the readiness of their talk. A great deal of wisdom and true worth may be with a slow tongue. God sometimes makes choice of these people as His messengers, who have the least advantages of art or nature, so that His grace in them may appear the more glorious.

Christ's disciples were no orators, until the Holy Spirit made them such. God condescends to answer the excuse of Moses. Even self-diffidence, when it stops us from or slows down our duty, is very displeasing to the Lord. But while we blame Moses for shrinking from this dangerous service, let us ask our own hearts if we are not neglecting duties easier and less perilous. The tongue of Aaron, with the head and heart of Moses, would make one completely fit for this errand.

God promises, I will be with your mouth and with his mouth. Even Aaron, who could speak well, yet could not speak to purpose, unless God gave constant teaching and help. For without the constant aid of Divine grace, the best gifts will fail.

-MATTHEW HENRY

When we turn to God for direction and obey Him, we too can demonstrate God's glory to the world like Moses did.

An Instrument of Peace

Do not present your members as instruments of unrighteousness to sin, but present yourselves to God as being alive from the dead, and your members as instruments of righteousness to God.
ROMANS 6:13 NKJV

Just as whoever loses their life for Christ will save it, the more we give to God, the more He gives of himself back. (See Mark 8:35 NIV.) The remarkably selfless prayer by Francis of Assisi (1181-1226) cries to God for us to be used for His glory.

> *Lord, make me an instrument of your peace:*
> *where there is hatred, let me sow love:*
> *where there is injury, pardon;*
> *where there is doubt, faith;*
> *where there is despair, hope;*
> *where there is darkness, light;*
> *and where there is sadness, joy.*
>
> *Divine Master, grant that I may not so much seek*
> *to be consoled as to console,*
> *to be understood as to understand,*
> *to be loved as to love.*
>
> *For it is in giving that we receive,*
> *it is in pardoning that we are pardoned,*
> *and it is in dying that we are born to eternal life.*
> -FRANCIS OF ASSISI

The more we give of ourselves to God, the more we will be able to give to others. And in serving God and others, we will find true joy.

"Christ died to save us, not from suffering, but from ourselves; not from injustice, far less from justice, but from being unjust."

-GEORGE MACDONALD

Peace with God's Forgiveness

Praise the Lord, O my soul . . . who forgives all your sins . . . who redeems your life from the pit and crowns you with love and compassion.
PSALM 103:2-4 NIV

There is an amazing sense of peace that comes with forgiveness. And the peace that God gives with His forgiveness has two parts. First, we have peace with ourselves, and second, we have peace with God. Andrew Murray reminds beginning Christians of the importance of living daily in this forgiveness.

The forgiveness of our sin is a complete forgiveness. God does not forgive by halves. Even with people, we consider half forgiveness no true forgiveness. The love of God is so great, and the atonement in the blood of Jesus so complete and powerful, that God always forgives completely. Take time with God's word to come under the full impression that your guilt has been blotted out wholly and altogether. God thinks absolutely no more of your sins. "I will forgive their wickedness and will remember their sins no more" (Jeremiah 31:34 NIV).

The forgiveness of our sin restores us entirely again to the love of God. Not only does God not blame us for sin any more—that is but one half—but He also gives to us the righteousness of Jesus also, so that for His sake we are as dear to God as He is. Not only is wrath turned away from us, but the fullness of love now rests upon us. "I will . . . love them freely, for my anger has turned away from them" (Hosea 14:4 NIV). Forgiveness is access to all the love of God. Forgiveness is also introduction to all the other blessings of redemption.

The forgiveness of former sins always gives us courage to go immediately anew with every new sin and trustfully to take forgiveness. Look, however, to one thing: the assurance of forgiveness must not be a matter of memory or understanding, but the fruit of life-living talk with the forgiving Father, with Jesus in whom we have forgiveness. It is not enough to know that I once received forgiveness: my life in the love of God, my living communication with Jesus by faith—this makes the forgiveness of sin again always new and powerful—the joy and the life of my soul.

-ANDREW MURRAY

The more time we spend in God's presence, the more aware we'll be of His glory and our unworthiness. Don't let this discourage you, but let it lift you up in thanksgiving. For God rescues us daily from our sin and gives us a new life in Him.

Blessed is he whose transgressions are forgiven, whose sins are covered.
PSALM 32:1 NIV

The Triumph of God's Good Purpose

We know that all things work together for good to those who love God, to those who are the called according to His purpose.
ROMANS 8:28 NKJV

The purpose or will of God is always good, always for our benefit. His blessings that sometimes come through bad circumstances are always worthwhile and satisfying. Saint Augustine writes of the amazing quality of God's will—that even when it seems negative, its purpose is good.

God achieves some of His purposes—which are, of course, all good—through the evil purposes of bad men. For example, it was through the ill will of the Jews that, by the good will of the Father, Christ was slain for us—a deed so good that when the apostle Peter would have nullified it he was called "Satan" by Him who had come in order to be slain. (See Matthew 16:23.)

How good the purposes of the [early Christians] seemed when they were unwilling that the apostle Paul should go to Jerusalem, for fear that there he should suffer the things that the prophet Agabus had predicted! (See Acts 21:10-12.) And yet God had willed that he should suffer these things for the sake of the preaching of Christ, and for the training of a martyr for Christ. And this good purpose of this He achieved, not through the good will of the Christians, but through the ill will of the Jews....

However strong the wills either of angels or of men, whether good or evil, whether they will the same as God or will the opposite, the will of the Omnipotent is always undefeated. And this purpose can never be evil, because even when it inflicts evils, it is still just; and obviously what is just is not evil. Therefore, whether through pity "He has mercy on whom He wills," or in justice "whom He wills, He hardens," the omnipotent God never does anything except what He does will, and does everything that He wills (Romans 9:18-19 NKJV).

-AUGUSTINE OF HIPPO

That God's will is always done frightens those of us who haven't experienced much of His loving character. However, think about Paul again. He wanted to follow God even into the danger in Jerusalem. He knew that God was a God of love and of mercy. God rescued him from the Jews, made him a prisoner of the Romans, but through it all Paul had the opportunity to testify to rulers and emperors just as God had planned. Don't think that the opposition of others in your life is the end of all good things that God can do. God can use the hostility of others to accomplish His will just as He can use your willing obedience. Do not despair. Trust in God's power to make everything work for Him—and for you!

It means for us all good,
All grace, all glory;
His Kingdom coming and on Earth begun.
Why should we fear to say,
"His Will, His righteous,
His tender loving, joyous Will be done!"?

-ANNIE JOHNSON FLINT

Trust and Peace

*You will keep him in perfect peace, whose mind is stayed on You,
because he trusts in You. Trust in the Lord forever, for in Yah,
the Lord, is everlasting strength.*
ISAIAH 26:3-4 NKJV

The more we trust God, the more we will be at peace and able to rest. When we trust Him, the creator of life and the ruler of the universe, we are safe and secure. God is in charge.

When we surrender and give Him control of our lives, He will bless us. This blessing may not be what we consider blessing. God will not keep us from problems or pain. But He will remain with us and give us peace, love, and hope. He is love.

Jesus surrendered to God and let God set Him on a path to what looked like certain death—and it was. But God was faithful and proved to Jesus and to us that even paths that lead through the curtain of death will not stop there in death. A kind of resurrection can take place in this place of trouble and dying, a resurrection to a new order of life that we could never have anticipated. And we would never experience it unless we were willing to let God lead us through difficult paths that sometimes seem to have nothing to recommend them. Our trust leads us with Jesus down into the valley of death and then upward and outward to a resurrection of our dreams and ourselves—and it only takes trusting God's goodness and faithfulness all the way through.

With God on our side, when we are surrendered to His will, we can only go forward!

The Purpose of the Bible

Your word is a lamp to my feet and a light to my path.
Psalm 119:105 NKJV

Why do we read the Bible? There are many reasons, practical and passionate. Like the Samaritan woman at the well, we thirst for living water. We hunger for every word that proceeds from the mouth of the Lord. John says that in the beginning was the Word. We read the Bible because not only does it guide and protect us, but it also is an immediate connection to the Word, God. Joanna Moore speaks of the vital necessity of reading the Bible, studying it, and responding to it also as a letter from God to us.

The Bible is a personal letter from God to His family on earth. Part of it is addressed to His saved children and part to those lost in sin; part to the weak and part to those who are stronger, and part to the faithful and part to the backslider. Then there is advice to children, to parents, to husband, to wife. There is a lesson in it for all, for every situation in life.

The devil does not care how much time you spend in prayer as long as you will not read the Bible. Because without the Bible you do not know how to pray an acceptable prayer.

I have never known a Christian to backslide who continued the daily, prayerful study of the Bible. Satan hates the Bible. It was the sword in Jesus' hands that conquered him nineteen hundred years ago. (See Matthew 4:1-11 and Ephesians 6:17.) Surely all Christians of every name should sit down together to read their Father's letter.

-JOANNA P. MOORE

When we sit down and read the Bible, the Holy Spirit will highlight and explain verses and stories. The Bible is personal because God is personal. He desires to have an intimate relationship with you. So sit down, pray for understanding, and read God's words to you.

Peace in God's Love

"Though the mountains be shaken and the hills be removed, yet my unfailing love for you will not be shaken nor my covenant of peace be removed," says the LORD, who has compassion on you.
ISAIAH 54:10 NIV

Many Christians fear that God will respond to our sins and doubt with frustration and anger, saying, "That's it! That's the last straw." Instead, God makes it clear that He won't ever stop loving His people—His sheep—even if they can't seem to trust and follow Him. Richard Baxter reassures us that we have no need to fear, because God's love is eternally constant.

Do not worry, dear soul. Be at peace. God's love is constant. It cannot be torn from you and it will never change except to grow stronger and stronger as you return it with love of your own.

You shall be eternally embraced in the arms of the love which was from everlasting and will extend to everlasting. This is the same love that brought the Son of God's love from heaven to earth, from earth to the cross, from the cross to the grave, from the grave to glory. It is the love through Christ which was weary, hungry, tempted, scorned, scourged, buffeted, spit upon, crucified, pierced; which did fast, pray, teach, heal, weep, sweat, bleed, and die. This love of God will eternally embrace you.

Let this be your everlasting comfort and peace, if God's

arms have once embraced you, neither sin nor hell can grip you. You do not have to deal with an inconstant human, but with Him with whom there is no variableness nor shadow of turning. His love to you will not be as yours is on earth to Him, seldom, and cold, up, and down. He will not cease nor reduce His love, for all your hostility, neglect, and opposition. How can He cease to love you, when He has made you truly lovely? He even keeps you so stable in your love to Him, that you can challenge all that will try to separate your love from Christ-tribulation, distress, persecution, famine, nakedness, peril, and sword. How much more will He himself be constant!

Indeed you should be "convinced that nothing—nothing living or dead, angelic or demonic, today or tomorrow, high or low, thinkable or unthinkable—absolutely nothing can get between us and God's love because of the way that Jesus our Master has embraced us" (Romans 8:38-39 MSG).

-RICHARD BAXTER

In Jesus for peace I abide,
And as I keep close to His side,
There's nothing but peace doth betide.
Sweet peace, the gift of God's love.
-PETER P. BILHORN

The Purpose and Blessing of Thanksgiving

Rejoice always, pray without ceasing, in everything give thanks; for this is the will of God in Christ Jesus for you.
1 THESSALONIANS 5:16-18 NKJ

It is hard to give thanks "in everything." There are so many bad things that we want to complain about. We find it hard to locate the blessings in both small annoyances and large evils. However, once we realize that God does constantly bless us, we will be able to thank Him for everything, including what we see as problems. Dwight Moody says that Paul suffered the most, but he was also the one who gave the most thanks to God.

Among all the apostles none suffered so much as Paul; but none of them do we find so often giving thanks as he. Remember what Paul suffered at Philippi; how they laid many stripes upon him, and cast him into prison. Yet every chapter in Philippians speaks of rejoicing and giving thanks. There is that well-known passage: "Be anxious for nothing, but in everything by prayer and supplication, with thanksgiving, let your requests be made known to God" (Philippians 4:6 NKJV).

-DWIGHT L. MOODY

It is hard at first to thank God for everything in prayer. But what may look like a problem to us is an opportunity for God to bless us.

God's blessing is exemplified in the history of Corrie ten Boom and her sister Betsie. While they were suffering in a concentration camp, Corrie was shocked when Betsie thanked God for the fleas that infested the barracks. Corrie could see no good in them, but her sister remained hopeful that God was blessing them with the fleas.

Weeks later they discovered that their freedom to hold prayer services in the middle of the day was because none of the guards wanted to be near the area while it was "crawling with fleas." Corrie realized they were "in the sanctuary of God's fleas."

Paul learned the same principle when he and Silas thanked God when they were in prison. They spent the night singing and praising God. Then God brought an earthquake, and their amazing example of faith converted both the other prisoners and the prison guard.

Let us remember to give thanks, because thanksgiving changes our heart and makes us realize the amazing grace that God continues to pour out on us.

> *I thank You for both smile and frown,*
> *And for the gain and loss;*
> *I praise You for the future crown,*
> *And for the present cross.*
> *I thank You for Your wings of love*
> *Which stir my worldly nest;*
> *And for the stormy clouds which drive me,*
> *Trembling, to Your breast.*
>
> -JANE FOX CREWDSON

The Purpose of God's Love

*Search me, O God, and know my heart; test me and know
my anxious thoughts. See if there is any offensive way in me,
and lead me in the way everlasting.*
PSALM 139:23-24 NIV

We are nothing in comparison to the Lord and His ways. And yet we are His beloved children. He loves us and enjoys spending time with us. This is the paradox that Evelyn Underhill addresses. We are nothing and yet, because of His love, we are worthy.

When we look out toward this love that moves the stars and stirs in the child's heart and claims our total allegiance, and remember that this alone is Reality and we are only real so far as we conform to its demands, we see our human situation from a fresh angle. We perceive that it is both more humble and dependent, and more splendid, than we had dreamed.

We are surrounded and penetrated by great spiritual forces of which we hardly know anything. Yet the outward events of our life cannot be understood, except in their relation to that unseen and intensely living world, the Infinite Goodness which penetrates and supports us, the God whom we resist and yet for whom we thirst; who is ever at work, transforming the self-centered desire of the natural creature into the wide spreading, outpouring love of the citizen of Heaven.

-Evelyn Underhill

Though we are presently saints, we are still being conformed to the image of Christ. As we serve Him and seek Him, God gransforms us by His presence. Ask God to change you into an overflowing channel of His love.

The Peace of Abiding in Christ in Prayer

*"If you abide in Me, and My words abide in you,
ask whatever you wish, and it will be done for you."*
JOHN 15:7 NASB

The concept of abiding in Christ is sometimes difficult. How do we abide or remain in Him when we have to move around and get things done? R. A. Torrey (1858-1928) says the secret of prayer is in this abiding. The following excerpt explains what and how to abide in Christ.

The whole secret of prayer is found in these words of our Lord. Here is prayer that has unbounded power: "Ask what you wish, and it will be done for you." There is a way then of asking and getting precisely what we ask and getting all we ask. Christ gives two conditions of this all-prevailing prayer. The first condition is, "If you abide in Me."

Now for us to abide in Christ is to bear the same relation to Him that branches bear to the vine. That is to say, to abide in Christ is to renounce any independent life of our own, to give up trying to think our thoughts, or form our resolutions, or cultivate our feelings, and simply and constantly look to Christ to think His thoughts in us, to form His purposes in us, to feel His emotions and affections in us. It is to renounce all life independent of Christ, and constantly to look to Him for the inflow of His life into us, and the outworking of His life through us. When we do this, and as much as we do this, our prayers will obtain what we seek from God.

This must necessarily be so, for our desires will not be our own desires, but Christ's, and our prayers will not in reality be our own prayers, but Christ praying in us. Such prayers will always be in harmony with God's will, and the Father hears them always.

-R. A. TORREY

The first steps to abiding in Christ are to read His Word and look to Him. As we seek God, He will change us and change others through us.

"The purpose of prayer is to release the power of God through us to accomplish the will of God on earth."

-DERK MADDEN

THE PURPOSE OF CHRIST-LIKE FORGIVENESS

[Jesus said,] "If you forgive men when they sin against you, your heavenly Father will also forgive you."
MATTHEW 6:14 NIV

God gives us the power to forgive and to go on forgiving. Corrie ten Boom survived the Holocaust and went on to start a ministry to other concentration camp survivors, both for former victims and also perpetrators. She found it hard work but didn't struggle much until she encountered a former camp guard who asked for her forgiveness. Her first response was anything but forgiveness. She then froze and told God that she couldn't forgive him, and that she needed help.

The following moment of love and forgiveness from God gave her this revelation: "So I discovered it is not on our forgiveness any more than on our goodness that the world's healing hinges, but on His. When He tells us to love our enemies, He gives, along with the command, the love itself."

The next story by Dwight L. Moody, gives an example of how Christ can give us the love and help to forgive.

Several years ago the Church of England sent a devoted missionary to New Zealand. One Sunday, after a few years of toil and success, he was holding a communion service in a district with many new converts. As the missionary was conducting the service, he observed one of the men, just as he was about to kneel at the rail, suddenly start to his feet and hastily go to the opposite end of the church. After a while he returned, and calmly took his place.

After the service the clergyman took him to the side, and asked the reason for his strange behavior. He replied, "As I was about to kneel I recognized in the man next to me the chief of a neighboring tribe, who had murdered my father and drunk his blood; and I had sworn by all the gods that I would slay that man at the first opportunity.

"The impulse to have my revenge, at first almost overpowered me, and I rushed away, as you saw me, to escape the power of it. As I stood at the other end of the room and considered the purpose of our meeting, I thought of Him who prayed for His own murderers, 'Father, forgive them, for they know not what they do.' And I felt then that I could forgive the murderer of my father, and I went and knelt down at his side."

-Dwight L. Moody

Christ's death on the cross was an amazing victory; it gave us forgiveness from God and the power to share that with those who hurt us. If you're struggling to forgive someone, ask God to give you the desire and ability to forgive them. He will give you the energy to take the next step.

"Forgiveness breaks the chain of causality because he who forgives you—out of love—takes upon himself the consequences of what you have done. Forgiveness, therefore, always entails a sacrifice."

-Dag Hammarskjöld

A Reason for Our Peace

God has called us to peace.
1 Corinthians 7:15 NKJV

As Christians, there are two reasons for our peace. God calls us to peace, and God's grace transforms us from fierce and bitter fighters to sweet and loving helpers. Thomas Watson writes of the wonders of God's grace that transforms us into His image.

It is the nature of grace to change the heart and make it peaceable. By nature we are of a fierce cruel disposition. When God cursed the ground for man's sake, the curse was that it should bring forth "thorns and thistles" (Genesis 3:18 NASB). The heart of man naturally lies under this curse. It brings forth nothing but the thistles of strife and contention.

But when grace comes into the heart it makes it peaceable. It infuses a sweet, loving disposition. It smoothes and polishes the most knotty piece. It files off the ruggedness in men's spirits.

Grace turns the vulture into a dove, the briar into a myrtle tree, the lion-like fierceness into a lamb-like gentleness. (See Isaiah 55:13.) "The wolf will dwell with the lamb, and the leopard will lie down with the young goat" (Isaiah 11:6-9 NASB). It is spoken of as the power which the gospel shall have upon men's hearts; it shall make such a metamorphosis that those who before were full of rage and antipathy shall now be made peaceable and gentle.

Peace shows us the character of a true saint. A saint is given to peace. They are the keeper of peace. The saint is "an heir of peace."

-THOMAS WATSON

We need not worry because we are constantly irritated, frustrated, impatient, and unable to be easygoing or nice. It is not our job to fix ourselves. We are to simply turn to God and ask Him to change us with His grace. He won't let us wallow in mud when we're meant to fly.

The Purpose of the Church—
to Be Led by Christ

> [Jesus said,] "Go therefore and make disciples of all the nations, baptizing them in the name of the Father and of the Son and of the Holy Spirit, teaching them to observe all things that I have commanded you; and lo, I am with you always, even to the end of the age."
> MATTHEW 28:19-20 NKJV

The purpose of the church is to seek out and do God's will, which is to train disciples, to heal the sick, and to reach the lost for His glory. We are to be a community demonstrating God's love. Andrew Murray writes how the plans for each church and for the greater church as a whole, should be carried out in obedience to God's specific plans for each congregation.

Some years ago, at Wellington, South Africa, where I live, we opened a Mission Institute. At our opening services the principal said something that I have never forgotten. He remarked:

"Last year we gathered here to lay the foundation stone, and what was there then to be seen? Nothing but rubbish, and stones, and bricks, and ruins of an old building that had been pulled down. There we laid the foundation stone, and very few knew what the building was that was to rise. No one knew it perfectly in every detail except one man, the architect. In his mind it was all clear, and as the contractor and the mason and the carpenter came to their work, they took their orders from him. The humblest laborer had to be obedient to orders. Therefore the structure rose, and this beautiful building has been completed. And just so," he added, "this building that we open today is but laying the foundation of a work of which only God knows what is to become."

But God has His workers and His plans clearly mapped out, and our position is to wait, that God should communicate to us as much of His will as each time is needful.

We have simply to be faithful in obedience, carrying out His orders. God has a plan for His Church upon earth. But alas, we too often make our plan, and we think that we know what ought to be done. We ask God first to bless our feeble efforts, instead of absolutely refusing to go unless God go before us.

God has planned for the work and the extension of His kingdom. The Holy Ghost has had that work given in charge to Him: "the work to which I have called them" (Acts 13:2 NKJV).

-ANDREW MURRAY

Just as individual Christians must learn to listen to God and obey Him, so it is for the Church. God will lead us and bless us as we seek Him individually and corporately. Let us ask Him what our next step is.

The Purpose of Revival

"If my people, who are called by my name, will humble themselves and pray and seek my face and turn from their wicked ways, then will I hear from heaven and will forgive their sin and will heal their land."

2 CHRONICLES 7:14 NIV

Revival is simply a turning back to God. When we pray for revival, we pray for people to change direction and to seek God's face. In the following sermon on revival, Billy Sunday (1862-1935) explains the need and purpose of revival.

A revival does two things. First, it returns the Church from her backsliding and second, it causes the conversion of men and women; and it always includes the conviction of sin on the part of the Church. A revival helps to bring the unsaved to Jesus Christ. God Almighty never intended that the devil should triumph over the Church.

When is a revival needed? When carelessness and unconcern keep the people asleep. It is as much the duty of the Church to awaken and work and labor for the men and women of this city as it is the duty of the fire department to rush out when the call sounds. What would you think of the fire department if it slept while the town burned? You would condemn them, and I will condemn you if you sleep and let men and women go to hell. It is just as much your business to be awake. The Church of God is asleep today; it is turned into a dormitory; and has taken the devil's sleeping pills.

When may a revival be expected? When the wickedness of the wicked grieves and distresses the Christian. Sometimes people don't seem to mind the sins of other people. Don't seem to mind while boys and girls walk the streets of their city and know more of evil than gray-haired men. We are asleep.

When is a revival needed? When the Christians have lost the spirit of prayer.

-BILLY SUNDAY

Oh, Lord, may we turn to You and weep for our sins and the sins of others. We are lost without Your Spirit and Your power. Send Your power, Lord.

Revive us, and we will call upon Your name. Restore us, O Lord God of hosts; cause Your face to shine, and we shall be saved!
PSALM 80:18-19 NKJV

"They tell me a revival is only temporary; so is a bath, but it does you good."

-BILLY SUNDAY

Peace of Conscience

[Jesus said,] "Produce fruit in keeping with repentance."
MATTHEW 3:8 NIV

Restitution, or making things right, is always a hard duty to face. However, the embarrassment, punishment, and pain we go through in admitting wrong and offering to fix things is more than overweighed by the feelings of peace and renewal once the problem has been faced. D. L. Moody tells the story of a man overwhelmed by guilt who finds the joy of forgiveness in restitution.

I was once preaching, and a man came up to me. He said, "I want you to notice that my hair is gray, and I am only thirty-two years old. For twelve years I have carried a great burden."

"Well," I said, "what is it?" He looked around as if afraid someone would hear him.

"Well," he answered, "my father died and left my mother with the county newspaper, and left her only that. That was all she had. After he died the paper began to waste away; and I saw my mother was fast sinking into a state of need. The building and the paper were insured for a thousand dollars, and when I was twenty years old I set fire to the building, and obtained the thousand dollars, and gave it to my mother. For twelve years that sin has been haunting me. I have tried to drown it by indulgence in pleasure and sin; I have cursed God; I have gone into infidelity; I have tried to make out that the

Bible is not true; I have done everything I could—but all these years I have been tormented."

I said, "There is a way out of that."

He inquired "How?"

I said, "Make restitution. Let us sit down and calculate the interest, and then you pay the company the money."

It would have done you good to see that man's face light up when he found there was mercy for him. He said he would be glad to pay back the money and interest if he could only be forgiven. There are men today who are in darkness and bondage because they are not willing to turn from their sins and confess them; and I do not know how a man can hope to be forgiven if he is not willing to confess his sin.

-D. L. MOODY

Prepare your confession and come back to GOD. Pray to him, "Take away our sin, accept our confession. Receive as restitution our repentant prayers."
HOSEA 14:2 MSG

The Purpose of the Body

"I do not pray for these alone, but also fo those who will believe in Me through their word; that they all may be one, as You, Father, are in Me, and I in You; that they also may be one in Us, that the world may believe that You sent Me. And the glory which You gave Me I have given them, that they may be one just as We are one."

JOHN 17:20-22 NKJV

One purpose of the body of Christ is for the members to strengthen each other. The unique gifts of each member build up the whole. The Puritan writer Thomas Watson shows how Christians build each other up with love by their mere contact.

One Christian conversing with another is a way to confirm them. As the stones in an arch help to strengthen one another, some Christians by imparting their experience, heat and quicken others. They "stimulate one another to love and good deeds," (Hebrews 10:24 NASB). How grace does flourish by holy discussion! A Christian by good conversation drops that oil upon another, which makes the lamp of their faith burn brighter.

Not only do Christians build each other up through talk, they also strengthen each other in prayer.

The saints pray for all the members of the Christian body, and their prayers prevail much. They prevail over recovery from sickness: "the prayer offered in faith will restore the one who is sick, and the Lord will raise him up" (James 5:15 NASB). They prevail for victory over enemies. When they offered "a prayer for the remnant that is left," then, "the angel of the Lord went out and struck 185,000 in the camp of the Assyrians" (Isaiah 37:4, 36 NASB).

They prevail for deliverance out of prison. "Prayer was made earnestly of the church unto God for him. . . . And behold an angel of the Lord stood by him, and a light shined in the cell: and he smote Peter on the side, and awoke him, . . . and his chains fell off" (Acts 12:5-7 ASV). The angel fetched Peter out of prison, but it was prayer that fetched the angel. And, they prevail for forgiveness of sin. "My servant Job will pray for you. For I will accept him" (Job 42:8 NASB).

Thus the prayers of the saints work for good to the Christian body.

—THOMAS WATSON

As part of the Christian body, we are tangible examples of God's love to each other and to the world. Keep encouraging and praying for others. It makes a difference.

The Purpose and Necessity of Emotions

Search me, O God, and know my heart;
test me and know my anxious thoughts.
PSALM 139:23 NIV

Affections, or feelings, often control what we do. Feelings can be logical, illogical, right, or wrong. Many people live by their emotions, swayed one way and then the other, barely in control of their own lives and living like they're a character in a soap opera. Other people make the opposite mistake of thinking, because feelings are sometimes unreliable, that they should distrust them altogether, and so they try to be cold and methodical like machines. Neither extreme is healthy, nor is it how God designed us to live. Jonathan Edwards (1703-1758) shows that the affections or emotions we experience are necessary because, as Christians, they can drive us onward to God's glory.

Such is our nature, that we are very inactive, unless we are influenced by some affection, either love or hatred, desire, hope, fear, or some other.

We see the world to be exceeding busy and active; and the affections of people are the springs of the motion: take away all love and hatred, all hope and fear, all anger, zeal, and affectionate desire, and the world would be, in a great measure motionless and dead; there would be no such thing as activity, or any earnest pursuit whatsoever.

It is affection that engages the covetous in their pursuits; and it is by the affections, that the ambitious are put forward in pursuit of worldly glory; and it is the affections also that motivate the voluptuous, in their pursuit of pleasure and sensual delights. The world continues from age to age in a continual commotion and agitation in a pursuit of these things. But take away all affection, and the spring of all this motion would be gone, and the motion itself would stop.

And just as in the world, worldly affections are very much the spring of men's motion and action; so in religion, the spring of their actions is very much religious affection. They that have doctrinal knowledge and theory without affection are never engaged in the business of religion.

-JONATHAN EDWARDS

Emotions are important, but so is obedience to an all-wise and loving God. The greatest commandment is "Love the Lord your God with all your heart, with all your soul, with all your mind, and with all your strength" (Mark 12:30 NKJV). It combines obedience with emotion. In 1 John 4, Paul says our love for God will be evident by our love for others. When we give our emotions over to God, He will turn them into love—His love.

The Purpose of Surrendering to Christ

Husbands, love your wives, just as Christ loved the church and gave himself up for her to make her holy, cleansing her by the washing with water through the word, and to present her to himself as a radiant church, without stain or wrinkle or any other blemish, but holy and blameless.

Ephesians 5:25-27 NIV

The purpose of our faith is to get us to take the step of obedience and let Christ take over and lead us. It is a step that feels a lot like dying to some, but also to finally living for others. Christ gave himself up for us and intends on purifying us and having us serve beside Him in joy. Hudson Taylor (1832-1905), in his amazing study on Song of Solomon, discusses the problem we have in fearing our Lord and Love even as we long for and wait for Him.

The Bridegroom is waiting for you all the time; the conditions that bar His approach are all of your own making. Take the right place before Him, and He will be most ready, most glad, to "Satisfy your deepest longings, to meet, supply your every need."

Could there be a sadder proof of the extent and reality of the Fall than the deep-seated distrust of our loving Lord and King which makes us hesitate to give ourselves entirely up to

Him, which fears that He might require something beyond our powers, or call for something that we should find it hard to give or to do? The real secret of an unsatisfied life lies too often in an unsurrendered will.

And yet how foolish, as well as how wrong, this is! Do we fancy that we are wiser than He? Or that our love for ourselves is more tender and strong than His? Or that we know ourselves better than He does? How our distrust must grieve and wound the tender heart of Him who was for us the Man of Sorrows! What would be the feelings of an earthly bridegroom if he discovered that his bride-elect was dreading to marry him, for fear that when he had the power, he should render her life miserable? Yet how many of the Lord's redeemed ones treat Him just so! No wonder they are neither happy nor satisfied! But true love cannot be stationary; it must either decline or grow.

Despite all the unworthy fears of our poor hearts, Divine love is destined to conquer.

-HUDSON TAYLOR

The Purpose of Spiritual Discipline

At the time, discipline isn't much fun. It always feels like it's going against the grain. Later, of course, it pays off handsomely, for it's the well-trained who find themselves mature in their relationship with God.
HEBREWS 12:11 MSG

A high school student once said Christian discipline is negative because it sounds like punishment. A more appropriate name for it would be Christian practices. But even with a simpler name, Christian disciplines can overwhelm and even distract us from our main purpose of hearing and responding to God.

One common misconception is that spiritual discipline itself is hearing from God. That it is all we need to have a healthy Christian life. However, spiritual discipline is necessary, but it is only the practice of a Christian life. We can be disciplined Christians and not hear the voice of God.

Hearing God's voice regularly and responding to it is the basis of Christianity. We study, pray, confess our sins, fast from food or other enjoyable treats, worship, memorize scripture, meditate, and sit in silence all for the purpose of learning to hear God's voice, to recognize it, and to have the strength to obey it. These disciplines are all vital to a Christian life, because we are still in training. Just as Jesus and the Father were one, we are to be one with them. (See John 17:21.) And we can't do that without constant practice and time learning how to be in God's presence.

Just as a musician practices scales to learn to play Mozart, we practice spiritual disciplines to learn to listen and obey God. We often think of discipline as difficult, mindless, and regimented activity. Our tired spirits wince at the thought of more hard work with little immediate payoff. Because we can still sometimes hear God without practicing spiritual disciplines, we take the easy way of occasional quiet times and weekly church attendance. However, without practicing scales, a musician can still play Mozart, but they cannot play well. And we won't hear God clearly and regularly if we aren't regularly practicing.

"For example, I fast from food to know that there is another food that sustains me. I memorize and meditate on scripture that the order of God's kingdom would become the order and power of my mind and my life."

-DALLAS WILLARD

Do not be discouraged. If you spend daily time reading Scripture and praying, you will hear from God; and He will give you the energy to continue with the other spiritual disciplines that will strengthen and tone your spiritual muscles so you can win the race.

Since we are surrounded by such a great cloud of witnesses, let us throw off everything that hinders and the sin that so easily entangles, and let us run with perseverance the race marked out for us.

HEBREWS 12:1 NIV

The Path of Peace

The meek shall inherit the earth,
and shall delight themselves in the abundance of peace.
PSALM 37:11 NKJV

The path of peace is humility. God will give us peace in the midst of great trials and chaos if we will humble ourselves to Him and trust that He wills good things for us. John Newton (1725-1807) says that God looks at our hearts rather than our outward actions. If we continue to seek Him, we will find Him and His everlasting peace.

One thing is needful; a humble, dependent spirit, to renounce our own wills, and give up ourselves to His disposal without reserve. This is the path of peace; and it is the path of safety; for He has said, the meek He will teach His way, and those who yield up themselves to Him He will guide with His eye (Psalm 25:9).... Jesus is a complete Savior, and we bring more honor to God by believing in His name and trusting His word of promise, than we could do by a thousand outward works.

-JOHN NEWTON

Stop worrying about what you have to do for God. Be still and know that He is God.

The Lord takes delight in his people; he crowns the humble with salvation.
PSALM 149:4 NIV

The Purpose of Joshua's Leadership

"No man shall be able to stand before you all the days of your life; as I was with Moses, so I will be with you. I will not leave you nor forsake you. . . . This Book of the Law shall not depart from your mouth, but you shall meditate in it day and night, that you may observe to do according to all that is written in it. For then you will make your way prosperous, and then you will have good success. Have I not commanded you? Be strong and of good courage; do not be afraid, nor be dismayed, for the Lord your God is with you wherever you go."

JOSHUA 1:5, 8-9 NKJV

We have both authority and power from God. The authority is in His words in the Bible, and the power is in the Holy Spirit that Jesus sent when He returned to Heaven. In Matthew Henry's commentary, he shows that Joshua was given all of God's power to lead the Israelites and to conquer other lands. But Joshua wasn't just to mimic Moses. Instead, Joshua was to study God's Word and live by it. God would give him both direction and power.

Joshua is to make the law of God his rule. He is charged to meditate in it day and night, so he might understand it. Whatever affairs of this world we have to mind, we must not neglect the one thing needful. All his orders to the people, and his judgments, must be according to the law of God. Joshua must himself be under command; no man's dignity or dominion sets him above the law of God. He is to encourage himself with the promise and presence of God.

Let not the sense of your own weakness discourage you; God is all-sufficient. I have commanded, called, and commissioned you to do it, and will be sure to abide with you in it. When we are in the way of duty, we have reason to be strong and very bold. Our Lord Jesus, as Joshua here, was borne up under his sufferings by a regard to the will of God, and the commandment from his Father.

-Matthew Henry

When we don't know what to do or where to go next, we can turn and ask God for direction as we read His Word.

The Purpose of Church

I long to see you so that I may impart to you some spiritual gift to make you strong—that is, that you and I may be mutually encouraged by each other's faith.
ROMANS 1:11-12 NIV

The unity that Christ shared with the Father is the same unity we are to have with other believers. (See John 17:21-23.) The church is a blessing and a gift from God. When believers spend time together, they encourage and sharpen each other. The outspoken evangelist Billy Sunday said the following in response to Christians who avoided church and other believers.

You say, "Mr. Sunday, I can be a Christian and go to heaven without joining a church." Yes, and you can go to Europe without getting on board a steamer. The swimming's good—but the sharks are laying in wait for those who take that route. I don't believe you. If someone is truly saved they will hunt for a church right away.

-BILLY SUNDAY

Spending time with other believers is as important as spending time with God and spending time reaching out to the lost. It keeps us safe and speeds us on our journey to become more like God. Be sure to have weekly opportunities to visit and learn from other Christians.

As iron sharpens iron, so one man sharpens another.
PROVERBS 27:17 NIV

THE PURPOSE OF MEDITATING ON SCRIPTURE FOR PRAYER

*My eyes are awake through the night watches,
that I may meditate on Your word.*
PSALM 119:148 NKJV

Have you ever tried to pray and found your mind wandering and your guilt, confusion, and chaos taking over rather than the peace of God? George Müller discovered that just as we hunger for breakfast in the morning, we also hunger for the Word of the Lord. He explains how he meditates on God's Word and how it leads naturally to prayer.

As our bodies are not fit for work for any length of time except with regular food, and as this is one of the first things we do in the morning, so it should be with our souls.

Now what is food for our souls? Not prayer, but the Word of God. And here again, it is not the simple reading of the Bible, so that it only passes through our minds, just as water runs through a pipe, but instead considering what we read, pondering over it and applying it to our hearts.

I began to meditate on the New Testament from the beginning, early in the morning. The first thing I did, after having asked in a few words the Lord's blessing on His precious Word, was, to begin to meditate on the Word of God. By meditate, I mean, searching every verse, to get blessing out of it . . . not for the sake of preaching on what I had read, but for the sake of obtaining food for my own soul. The result I have found to be almost always this, that after a very few minutes my soul has been led to confession, or to thanksgiving, or to intercession, or to supplication; so that, though I did not give myself to prayer, but to meditation, yet it turned almost immediately more or less into prayer.

When I have been praying for a while, I go on to the next words or verse, turning all, as I go on, into prayer for myself or others, as the Bible may lead to it. But I still continually keep before me that my purpose for meditation is food for my own soul. The result of this is that there is always a good deal of confession, thanksgiving, supplication, or intercession mingled with my meditation, and that my soul is almost always nourished and strengthened. By breakfast time, with rare exceptions, I am in a peaceful if not happy state of heart.

-GEORGE MÜLLER

When we have a daily breakfast of Scripture, we are ready, willing, and able to notice and join in God's working in our lives and the lives around us.

The Peace of Friendship

No test or temptation that comes your way is beyond the course of what others have had to face. All you need to remember is that God will never let you down; he'll never let you be pushed past your limit; he'll always be there to help you come through it.

1 CORINTHIANS 10:13 MSG

The friendship of the poet William Cowper and the *Amazing Grace* writer and pastor John Newton was one of strength and hope. Cowper suffered from depression and illness most of his life. He was unable to hold a job but spent his time writing. Many times when he suffered greatly from depression and contemplated suicide, his friend Newton would be there to pull him back to safety.

They wrote hymns together that still encourage Christians today. Their poetry and hymns are moving because they wrote from their own experience with doubt, fear, and the saving hope of Christ. The following hymn by John Newton can give us confidence that no matter what trials or problems we encounter, God is good, and He will provide the strength and encouragement to continue.

> *Though troubles assail us and dangers affright,*
> *Though friends should all fail us and foes all unite,*
> *Yet one thing secures us, whatever betide,*
> *The promise assures us, "The Lord will provide."*

When Satan assails us to stop up our path,
And courage all fails us, we triumph by faith.
He cannot take from us, though oft he has tried,
This heart cheering promise, "The Lord will provide."

He tells us we're weak, our hope is in vain,
The good that we seek we never shall obtain,
But when such suggestions, our graces have tried,
This answers all questions, "The Lord will provide."

No strength of our own and no goodness we claim;
Yet, since we have known of the Savior's great Name,
In this our strong tower for safety we hide:
The Lord is our power, "The Lord will provide."

When life sinks a pace, and death is in view,
The word of His grace shall comfort us through,
Not fearing or doubting, with Christ on our side,
We hope to die shouting, "The Lord will provide."
—JOHN NEWTON

God will provide. Just as He gave William Cowper the encouragement and friendship of John Newton, He will provide for you. If you're lonely and there is no friend in sight, it's because He wants you close to Him. He will be the friend you can count on.

The Purpose of the Trinity

[Jesus said,] "I and the Father are one."
John 10:30 NIV

Someone once said that the only way for God to be love is for God to be more than one being. With the relationship between the Father, the Son, and the Holy Spirit, God can continually be love and love us. The following creed explores the amazing nature of the Trinity that brings life to each of us.

We worship one God in trinity and the trinity in unity, neither blending their persons nor dividing their essence.

For the person of the Father is a distinct person, the person of the Son is another, and that of the Holy Spirit still another.

But the divinity of the Father, Son, and Holy Spirit is one, their glory equal, their majesty co-eternal. What quality the Father has, the Son has, and the Holy Spirit has. The Father is uncreated, the Son is uncreated, the Holy Spirit is uncreated. The Father is immeasurable, the Son is immeasurable, the Holy Spirit is immeasurable. The Father is eternal, the Son is eternal, the Holy Spirit is eternal.

And yet there are not three eternal beings; there is but one eternal being.

So too there are not three uncreated or immeasurable beings; there is but one uncreated and immeasurable being. Similarly, the Father is almighty, the Son is almighty, the Holy Spirit is almighty. Yet there are not three almighty beings; there is but one almighty being. Thus the Father is God, the Son is God, the Holy Spirit is God.

Yet there are not three gods; there is but one God. Thus the Father is Lord, the Son is Lord, the Holy Spirit is Lord. Yet there are not three lords; there is but one Lord.

The Father was neither made nor created nor begotten from anyone. The Son was neither made nor created; he was begotten from the Father alone. The Holy Spirit was neither made nor created nor begotten; he proceeds from the Father and the Son. Accordingly there is one Father, not three fathers; there is one Son, not three sons; there is one Holy Spirit, not three holy spirits. Nothing in this trinity is before or after, nothing is greater or smaller; in their entirety the three persons are co-eternal and co-equal with each other.

So in everything, as was said earlier, we must worship their trinity in their unity and their unity in their trinity.

-ATHANASIAN CREED

Just as the purpose of God is love, the purpose of the Trinity is love. The Father longs for a relationship with us that is as close as His relationship with Jesus and the Holy Spirit. May we open our hearts wide for His embrace and accept the love that He gives.

[Jesus said,] "The glory which You have given Me I have given to them, that they may be one, just as We are one; I in them and You in Me, that they may be perfected in unity, so that the world may know that You sent Me, and loved them, even as You have loved Me."

JOHN 17:22-23 NASB

God's Purposes for Us Aren't Always Logical

"Not by might nor by power, but by My Spirit," says the Lord of hosts.
ZECHARIAH 4:6 NASB

When men and women are called to do God's work, they know He called them. But many times the others around them don't feel that call and cannot understand what would make their friends take such a crazy leap. Many missionaries and preachers started out shy, unable to speak in front of audiences, without training, without going to seminary. Gladys Aylward (1904-1970) left England for China when she was twenty-six. She had only three months of training before the school decided she was unqualified for a trip to China. Gladys saved her money and went alone by train through communist Russia and walked over the Siberian border for the first part of her journey.

Once she was there, she was able to learn the language and to affect everyone around her by her servant's heart. She took in over 100 orphans and nursed Chinese soldiers during the war with Japan. The people loved her, and many turned to Christ because of her presence. She said about her life: "My heart is full of praise that one so insignificant, uneducated, and ordinary in every way could be used to His glory for the blessing of His people in poor persecuted China."

Amy Carmichael (1867-1951) went to be a missionary in India and was there for fifty-six years. She was sick with neuralgia often for weeks on end, but she felt drawn to missions and serving the lost. Amy was best known for taking in and sheltering girls whose parents had given them up to be temple prostitutes.

As a child, she had longed for blue eyes like her Irish parents. But Amy's brown eyes were a perfect disguise when she snuck into temples, kidnapped, and saved girls from lives of prostitution and poverty. She was content to be serving God in whatever position He allowed. She said, "If I cannot in honest happiness take the second place (or the twentieth); if I cannot take the first without making a fuss about my unworthiness, then I know nothing of Calvary love."

God often picks the humble and lowly to do His work. If we have no confidence in ourselves, but rest in God's power, then we can do anything.

> *"You can give without loving,
> but you cannot love without giving."*
> -AMY CARMICHAEL

The Purpose of Spiritual Power Is Holiness

Hope does not disappoint us, because God has poured out his love into our hearts by the Holy Spirit, whom he has given us.
ROMANS 5:5 NIV

One of the main reasons for spiritual power through the Holy Spirit is the need to be holy. As humans we have a natural tendency to sin. We may train ourselves to not outwardly sin, but it is difficult to change our hearts. This is what the power of Christ is for. Not only are we to heal the sick and cast out demons, but we are to love others with the forgiving and saving love of Christ.

We cannot act in this love without the Spirit of Christ and without His power. The following excerpt by the Puritan Jonathon Edwards explains why we need changed hearts filled with joy and energy to follow Christ and do His will.

We are nothing if we do not practice Christianity with earnest hearts; and our wills and inclinations are not strongly exercised. The things of Christianity are so great, that there can be no suitableness in the exercises of our hearts, to their nature and importance, unless they are lively and powerful. In nothing is vigor in our actions and inclinations so necessary, as in Christianity; and in nothing is lukewarmness so odious.

True Christianity is increasingly a powerful thing; and the power of it appears, in the first place in the inward exercises of it in the heart, where the principal and original seat of it is. Therefore true religion is called the power of godliness. This is in distinction from the external appearances of it that are only the form of it, like in 2 Timothy 3:5, "Having a form of godliness, but denying the power of it" (NIV).

In those that have sound and solid Christian faith, the Spirit of God is a spirit of powerful holy affection. Therefore, God is said to have given us "a spirit of power, of love and of self-discipline" (2 Timothy 1:7 NIV). When we receive the Spirit of God with His sanctifying and saving influences, we are said to be "baptized with the Holy Ghost, and with fire" because the power and fervor of those exercises the Spirit of God excites in our hearts. And our hearts, when grace is in use, may be said to "burn within"; as is said of the disciples. (See Luke 24:32.)

-JONATHAN EDWARDS

Don't be intimidated by the thought of being a saint. God has cleansed us from sin and given us His Holy Spirit—His presence that brings the ability to conquer sin and live for God.

Assurance and Peace

Faith is the assurance of things hoped for, the conviction of things not seen.
HEBREWS 11:1 NASB

The assurance of the love of God, of the salvation through Christ, and the power of the Holy Spirit to overcome sin changes our lives. We live in confidence and authority. Charles Spurgeon demonstrates how this assurance is the driving force behind active Christian lives.

A well-grounded assurance is the most active worker in the field, the most valiant warrior in the battle, and the most patient sufferer in the furnace. There are none as active as the assured. Let a tree be planted in this soil, and watered with this river, and its boughs will bend with fruit. Confidence of success stimulates exertion, joy in faith removes sorrows, and realizing assurance overcomes all difficulties.... What does the tempest without matter when there is calm within?

Assurance puts the heart in heaven, and moves the feet to heaven.... There never were souls so self-sacrificing, so daring, so zealous, so enthusiastic in the cause of Christ, as the ones who know that their names were written in the Lamb's Book of Life, and therefore out of gratitude serve their God.

Spurgeon wonders why anyone would think that someone

secure in their love for Christ would want to return to their life of sin away from the Savior. He tells us to think of our lives before Christ and how amazing His offer of grace and forgiveness was. We would immediately reply to God's calling with: "I would do anything for Him; I would live for Him; I would die for Him, to show how I love Him who loved me."

Spurgeon responds to the sinner's cry of love and devotion with the following promise.

Oh, poor soul, if you believe in Christ now, that will be true. If you will cast yourself on Jesus, you shall be forgiven. There shall be no sin left in God's book against you. You shall be absolved, acquitted, delivered, cleansed and washed; and then you shall prove in your experience that assurance does not make men sin, but that assurance of pardon is the very best means of making men holy, and keeping them in the fear of God.

-CHARLES H. SPURGEON

The Purpose of Christ's Judgment for Christians

Whoever lives in love lives in God, and God in him. In this way, love is made complete among us so that we will have confidence on the day of judgment, because in this world we are like him.

1 JOHN 4:16-17 NIV

How often we fear the day when Jesus returns because we think He will chide us for our many mistakes and omissions. Richard Baxter argues forcefully against our fear, demonstrating how God's perfect love for us should send our fear away.

What inexpressible joy, that our dear Lord, who loves our souls and whom our souls love, shall be our Judge! Will a man fear to be judged by his best friend, or a wife by her own husband? Did Christ come down and suffer, weep, bleed, and die for you, and will He then condemn you? Was He judged, condemned, and executed in your place, and now will He himself condemn you? Has He done most of the work already, in redeeming, regenerating, sanctifying and preserving you, and will He now undo it all again? Well then, let your terror of the day of judgment decrease. Surely our Lord can mean no harm to us at all. Let that day make the devils and the wicked tremble, but let it make us leap for joy.

-RICHARD BAXTER

You might say, "Yes, but we are supposed to be living differently, and I have some things I just can't seem to overcome." Have no fear, child of God, He knows your every struggle and has promised that this, too, He will give to you—the power to overcome each difficulty as you grow in the knowledge of His love and grace. The apostle Paul promises, "Faithful is He who calls you, and He also will bring it to pass" (1 Thessalonians 5:24 NASB). First rest in His love to save you from sin; then learn to rest in His great love and power to save you from sin's present dominion over your life. In every case, the secret of peace and an eagerness for the appearing of Jesus is to rest in Him.

The Day of Judgment holds no fear for the Christian. For them, it will be a day of great rejoicing and praise. Christ will come in all His glory and claim all believers as His very own children!

Are you ready for the coming of the Lord from heav'n?
Are you resting in the promise which to us is giv'n?
Does your heart leap up with rapture as you know He's near?
Or do thoughts of His appearing fill your heart with fear?
    -ADA R. HABERSHON

Peace with Doubts

Plead my cause, O Lord, with those who strive with me; fight against those who fight against me. Take hold of shield and buckler, and stand up for my help. Also draw out the spear, and stop those who pursue me. Say to my soul, "I am your salvation."

PSALM 35:1-3 NKJV

We often have doubts that assail and attack, making it hard for us to remain calm and assured with the love and control of God. Charles Spurgeon reassures us that in the Bible it says that David doubted, but that he turned to God with his doubts, and God answered him.

The first thing Psalm 35 seems to say is that David had his doubts. For why would he pray, "Say to my soul, I am your salvation," if he were not sometimes overcome with doubts and fears? Cheer up, fellow Christian! If David doubted, you must not say, "I am no Christian, because I have doubts."

The strongest of Christians are sometimes troubled with fears and anxieties. Abraham had the greatest faith, but he had some unbelief. I envy the one who can say that their faith never wavered. They can say more than David did, for David had cause to cry, "Say to my soul, I am your salvation."

But, next, Psalm 35 says that David was not content while he had doubts and fears, but he went at once to the mercy-seat to pray for assurance, for he valued it as much fine gold. "O

Lord!" David seems to say, "I have lost my confidence; my foot slips; my feet are almost gone; my doubts and fears prevail; but I cannot bear it. I am wretched, I am unhappy. 'Say, say to my soul, I am your salvation.'"

And then the text tells you a third thing—that David knew where to obtain full assurance. He goes at once to God in prayer. He knows that knee-work is what increases faith. It is there, in his closet, that he cries out to the Most High, "Say to my soul, I am your salvation."

Oh my brethren, we must be often alone with God if we are to have a clear sense of His love! Let your cries cease, and your eyes will grow dim. Much in prayer, much in heaven; slow in prayer, slow in progress.

-CHARLES H. SPURGEON

We too must turn to God with our doubts and fears. Our Heavenly Father is "the God of all comfort" (2 Corinthians 1:3). He will give us peace.

The Purposes of God's Promises

As we know Jesus better, his divine power gives us everything we need for living a godly life. He has called us to receive his own glory and goodness! And by that same mighty power, he has given us all of his rich and wonderful promises.

2 PETER 1:3-4 NLT

When we know and depend on God's promises, we are standing on the strength of God's character. The Puritan writer Thomas Watson speaks of God's promises in the Bible as food and as springs of joy. They encourage, strengthen, and give us hope to trust God and to do His work.

How do the promises work for good? They are food for faith; and that which strengthens faith works for good. The promises are the milk of faith; faith sucks nourishment from them, as the child from the breast.

"Jacob was greatly afraid" (Genesis 32:7 NASB). His spirits were ready to faint; now he goes to the promise, "For you have said, 'I will surely prosper you'" (Genesis 32:12 NASB). This promise was his food. He got so much strength from this promise, that he was able to wrestle with the Lord all night in prayer, and would not let Him go till He had blessed him.

The promises also are springs of joy. . . . The promises are as cork to the net, to bear up the heart from sinking in the deep waters of distress.

-THOMAS WATSON

The Purpose of Abiding in Prayer

[Jesus said,] "If you abide in Me, and My words abide in you, ask whatever you wish, and it will be done for you."
JOHN 15:7 NASB

When we abide and spend time in Christ, our prayers become powerful. And the way to abide in Christ is to read and know His Word. We must live and breathe God's Word. It is our life and our food. R. A. Torrey says when we dwell in Christ and His Word, we will naturally know the right things to pray for, and we will have power when we pray.

If we are to obtain from God all that we ask from Him, Christ's words must abide or continue in us. We must study His words, fairly devour His words, let them sink into our thought and into our heart, keep them in our memory, obey them constantly in our life, let them shape and mold our daily life and our every act.

This is really the method of abiding in Christ. It is through His words that Jesus imparts himself to us. The words He speaks unto us, they are spirit and they are life. (See John 6:63.) It is vain to expect power in prayer unless we meditate much upon the words of Christ, and let them sink deep and find a permanent home in our hearts.

It is not by times of mystical meditation and rapturous experiences that we learn to abide in Christ; it is by feeding upon His word, His written word as found in the Bible, and looking to the Holy Spirit to plant these words in our hearts and to make them a living thing in our hearts.

If we then let the words of Christ abide in us, they will stir us up in prayer. They will be the mold in which our prayers are shaped, and our prayers will be necessarily along the line of God's will, and will triumph with Him. Triumphant prayer is almost impossible where there is neglect of the study of the Word of God.

George Müller, one of the mightiest men of prayer of the present generation, would begin by reading and meditating upon God's Word until out of the study of the Word a prayer began to form itself in his heart. Thus God himself was a real author of the prayer, and God answered the prayers which He himself had inspired.

-R. A. TORREY

May we also begin prayer by reading God's Word and praying and responding to it as God prompts us.

[Jesus said,] "These things I have spoken to you so that My joy may be in you, and that your joy may be made full."
JOHN 15:11 NASB

God's Eternal Purpose

Be exalted, O God, above the heavens; let your glory be over all the earth.
PSALM 57:11 NIV

God's glory is not just for His own benefit. He is a wise, powerful, and loving God, so we also benefit from His glory. John Calvin (1509-1564) writes that God's eternal purpose is His glory and therefore our glory.

What is God's purpose in creation and what is His purpose in redemption? It may be summed up in two phrases, one from each of our two sections of Romans. It is: "The glory of God" (Romans 3:23 KJV), and "The glory of the children of God" (Romans 8:21 KJV).

In Romans 3:23 we read: "All have sinned, and fall short of the glory of God." God's purpose for humans was glory, but sin thwarted that purpose by causing humans to miss God's glory. When we think of sin we instinctively think of the judgment it brings; we invariably associate it with condemnation and hell. Our thought is always of the punishment that will come to us if we sin.

But God's thought is always of the glory we will miss when we sin. The result of sin is that we forfeit God's glory: the result of redemption is that we are qualified again for glory. God's purpose in redemption is glory, glory, glory.

-JOHN CALVIN

Let us rejoice and praise God for His amazing purpose that includes us in His glory and joy!

The Wisdom of Peace

I, wisdom, dwell together with prudence; I possess knowledge and discretion. To fear the Lord is to hate evil; I hate pride and arrogance, evil behavior and perverse speech. Counsel and sound judgment are mine; I have understanding and power.

PROVERBS 8:12-14 NIV

It is wise to be at peace with oneself and with others. To bring peace is to be at peace. It is a circular cause-and-effect situation. If we have inner peace, we will bring peace to others. If others are at peace, we will gain peace from them in return. Thomas Watson, a writer from the 1600s, writes of God's wisdom bringing peace: peace to us and peace to those around us.

To be a peaceable spirit is highly prudent. "The wisdom from above is . . . peaceable" (James 3:17 NKJV). A wise man will not meddle with strife. It is like putting one's finger into a hornets' nest—or to use Solomon's example, "the beginning of strife is like releasing water" (Proverbs 17:14 NKJV). To seek out the folly of strife is like releasing water in two respects. First, when water begins to be let out there is no end of it. So there is no end of strife when once begun. Second, the letting out of water is dangerous.

If a person should break down a bank and let in an arm of the sea, the water might overflow their fields and drown them in the flood. It is the same with those that meddle with strife. They may cause mischief to themselves and open such a current that may engulf and swallow them up. True wisdom promotes peace. The prudent will keep away from conflict as much as they can.

To be of a peaceable spirit brings peace along with it. The contentious annoy themselves and destroy their own comfort. They are like the bird that beats itself against the cage. The wicked one "troubles his own flesh" (Proverbs 11:17 NKJV). They are just like one that cuts off the sweet of the apple and eats nothing but the core. So a quarrelsome person cuts off all the comfort of their life and feeds only upon the bitter core of unrest. They are self-tormentors. The wicked are compared to "a troubled sea" (Isaiah 57:20 NKJV). And it follows "there is no peace . . . for the wicked" (verse 21). The Septuagint renders it "There is no joy to the wicked."

Pushy people do not enjoy what they possess, but the peace-loving spirit brings the sweet music of peace along with them. It makes a calm and harmony in the soul. Therefore the psalmist says, it is not only good, but pleasant, to live together in unity. (See Psalm 133:1.)

-THOMAS WATSON

God, is there any area of my life in which I'm unwisely tempted to release the swirling waters of a quarrel? I ask for Your wisdom to be a gentle peacemaker.

The Purpose of the Holy Spirit Is to Teach

"The Helper, the Holy Spirit, whom the Father will send in My name, He will teach you all things, and bring to your remembrance all that I said to you."

JOHN 14:26 NASB

Not only is the Holy Spirit necessary for the power to do God's will, but He also delights in teaching us God's Word and character. The Holy Spirit is our personal tutor and our author's commentary on the Bible. All that is necessary for learning and understanding God's Word is a willing heart and some time spent quietly reading and asking God what He means. George Müller, the preacher and orphanage starter, learned that the best way to understand God's Word is from God himself.

God began to show me that his word alone is our standard of judgment in spiritual things; that it can be explained only by the Holy Spirit; and that in our day as well as in former times, He is the teacher of his people. . . . And, further, that the Holy Spirit alone can teach us about our state by nature, show us the need of a Savior, enable us to believe in Christ, explain to us the Scriptures, help us in preaching, etc.

When I began to understand this latter point, it had a great effect on me. The Lord enabled me to put it to the test of experience, by laying aside commentaries, and almost every other book, and simply reading the word of God and studying it. The result was, that the first evening that I shut myself into my room, to give myself to prayer and meditation over the Scriptures, I learned more in a few hours than I had done during a period of several months previously. But the particular difference was, that I received real strength for my soul in doing so.

-GEORGE MÜLLER

O, God, may we seek and learn to understand all about You in Your Word. Give us the courage to daily spend time reading the Bible and listening for the message You have for us.

A Purpose for the Lost

[Jesus said,] "The Son of man came to seek and save that which was lost."
LUKE 19:10 ASV

There are people who make a difference for God. They take risks, give their all, and change the world—not for themselves, but for God. If we are to make the most of every opportunity, it would be good to look at the life of Dwight L. Moody, who was so focused on saving lives and preaching the Gospel that he was infamous in his city of Chicago.

Once, when walking down a certain street in Chicago, Mr. Moody stepped up to a man, a perfect stranger to him, and said, "Sir, are you a Christian?"

"You mind your own business," was the reply.

Mr. Moody replied, "This is my business."

The man said, "Well, then, you must be Moody." Out in Chicago they used to call him in those early days "Crazy Moody," because day and night he was speaking to everybody he got a chance to speak to about being saved.

On one occasion in Chicago, Mr. Moody saw a little girl standing on the street with a pail in her hand. He went up to her and invited her to his Sunday school, telling her what a pleasant place it was. She promised to go the following Sunday, but she did not do so. Mr. Moody watched for her for weeks, and then one day he saw her on the street again, at some distance from him. He started toward her, but she saw him too and started to run away. Mr. Moody followed her.

Down she went one street, Mr. Moody after her; up she went another street, Mr. Moody after her, through an alley, Mr. Moody still following; out on another street, Mr. Moody after her; then she dashed into a saloon and Mr. Moody dashed after her. She ran out the back door and up a flight of stairs, Mr. Moody still following; she dashed into a room, Mr. Moody following; she threw herself under the bed and Mr. Moody reached under the bed and pulled her out by the foot, and led her to Christ.

-R. A. TORREY

These anecdotes show how energetic and humble Moody was. He chased after the girl like Christ sought for His lost lamb—with determination and love. Be encouraged by Moody's example. The last few things Christ told Peter was, "Take care of my sheep. Feed my sheep. Follow Me." (See John 21:16-19.) And we shall follow Him too.

> *Going afar*
> *Upon the mountain*
> *Bringing the wanderer back again*
> *Into the fold*
> *Of my Redeemer*
> *Jesus the Lamb for sinners slain*
> -WILLIAM A. OGDEN

INNER PEACE

"I've told you all this so that trusting me, you will be unshakable and assured, deeply at peace. In this godless world you will continue to experience difficulties. But take heart! I've conquered the world."
JOHN 16:33 MSG

There are some who seem to have an inner peace that takes no notice of the problems and chaos surrounding them. These pure souls haven't lost the ability to care for others, but their inward focus on God maintains and continues to give them strength during both normal everyday busyness and the abnormal crisis. The writer of the Theologia Germanica tells of the inward peace that Christ promises with the reminder that He has overcome the world.

Many say they have no peace or rest, but instead suffer so many crosses and trials, problems and sorrows, that they don't know how they'll ever get through them. Now those who are wise know that true peace and rest doesn't lie in outward things. If it did, Satan could have peace when things go according to his will. This is not the case; for the scriptures declare there is no peace for the wicked. (See Isaiah 57:21 NKJV.)

And therefore we must consider and see what kind of peace Christ left to His disciples when He said, "Peace I leave with you, My peace I give to you" (John 14:27 NKJV). We may see that in these words Christ did not mean an outward peace, for His disciples with all His friends and followers have suffered great affliction, persecution, and often martyrdom. Christ himself said, "In the world you will have tribulation" (John 16:33 NKJV).

But Christ gave the true, inward peace of the heart, which begins here on earth, and endures forever. Therefore He said, "not as the world gives," for the world is false, and deceives in its gifts. It promises much, and achieves little. Moreover there lives no one on earth who will always have rest and peace without troubles and crosses. There is always something to be suffered here. And as soon as you are done with one attack, perhaps two come in its place. Therefore yield yourself willingly to them, and only seek that true peace of the heart, which none can take away from you, that you may overcome all attacks.

Christ gives that inward peace which can break through all attacks and crosses of oppression, suffering, misery, and humiliation, so that we can be joyful and patient in the midst of it. Now those who will in love give their whole diligence and might, will truly come to know that true eternal peace which is God himself, as far as it is possible to a creature. What was bitter to them before, shall become sweet, and their heart shall remain unmoved under all outward changes, and they shall attain everlasting peace.

-THEOLOGIA GERMANICA

And it is God himself who is our peace that we seek. He soothes us as a mother does a child. In His presence we know that He is in charge and all will be well.

"All God wants of one is a peaceful heart."
-MEISTER ECKHART

Comfort in God Alone

Blessed be the God and Father of our Lord Jesus Christ, the Father of mercies and God of all comfort.
2 CORINTHIANS 1:3 NASB

It can be difficult for us to desire the eternal rewards of Heaven over the present enticements of earth. Time is fleeting. We have to endure only for a short while, so resisting temptation should be easy. The wealth of earth is worthless compared to Heaven's treasure, but we still struggle against the preoccupation with wealth and stuff.

Thomas à Kempis explains that even if you have all of life's pleasures, they will not satisfy because nothing can complete us like Christ.

My soul, you cannot enjoy full consolation or perfect delight except in God, the Consoler of the poor and the Helper of the humble. Wait a little, and you will have an abundance of all good things in heaven. If you desire these present things of the world too much, you will lose those which are everlasting and heavenly. You cannot be satisfied with any earthly things because you were not created to enjoy them.

And even if you possessed all created things you could not be happy; for your whole happiness consists in God, who created all these things. This happiness is not the type that the world understands. It is the kind that the faithful servants of Christ can sometimes touch. It is the presence of God.

If you are sad, remember all human comfort is vain and brief. But the comfort from God is blessed and true. The devout person carries their Consoler, Jesus, everywhere with them, and they say to Him: "Be with me, Lord Jesus, in every place and at all times. Let this be my consolation, to be willing to do without all human comforting. Let Your will and just trial of me be my greatest comfort."

-THOMAS À KEMPIS

This world is not my home, I'm just a passing through;
My treasures are laid up somewhere beyond the blue.

-J. R. BAXTER, JR.

A Purpose for Depression

*[God] comes alongside us when we go through hard times,
and before you know it, he brings us alongside someone else who is going
through hard times so that we can be there for that person
just as God was there for us.*
2 CORINTHIANS 1:4 MSG

God always has a reason for the bad times or pain we go through. Usually God is attempting to bless us or teach us something, but other times He uses us to reach others. Charles Spurgeon tells of a time when he was depressed and full of darkness, and how God used this to help another.

One Sabbath morning, I preached from the text, "My God, My God, why have You forsaken Me?" and though I did not say so, I preached my own experience. I heard my own chains clank while I tried to preach to my fellow-prisoners in the dark. I could not tell why I was brought into such an awful horror of darkness, instead I condemned myself.

On the following Monday evening, a man came to see me who bore all the marks of despair upon his face. His hair seemed to stand upright, and his eyes were ready to start from their sockets. He said to me, after a little while, "I have never before in my life heard any man speak who seemed to know my heart. Mine is a terrible case; but on Sunday morning you pointed me to the life and preached as if you had been inside my soul."

By God's grace, I saved that man from suicide and led him into gospel light and liberty. I know I could not have done it if I had not myself been confined in the dungeon in which he lay. I tell the story, because you sometimes may not understand your own experience, and the perfect people around you may condemn you for having it; but what do they know of God's servants?

We have to suffer much for the sake of the people of our charge. God's sheep ramble very far, and we have to go after them. Sometimes the shepherds go where they themselves would never roam if they weren't in pursuit of lost sheep. You may be in darkness, and you may wonder why such a horror chills your marrow; but you may be altogether in the pursuit of your calling, and be led of the Spirit to a position of sympathy with despairing minds. Expect to grow weaker, that you may comfort the weak.

-CHARLES SPURGEON

God is a God of mercy and understanding. As Christ, He died on the cross and rose again to first conquer sin and pain, but second to feel how lost and lonely and miserable we are when we are without the saving love that is God. He lived the death we live, and then He rose again and gave us a new life.

Peace for the Doubting Christian

God split the rocks in the desert and gave them water as abundant as the seas; he brought streams out of a rocky crag and made water flow down like rivers.

Psalm 78:15-16 NIV

The water images in the Bible imply the plentitude of the Lord. The one whose delight is in the law of the Lord is like a tree planted by streams of water. (See Psalm 1:2-3.) Those who drink the water of Christ will never thirst. (See John 4:14.) Indeed, He will bless and bless again His followers—not based on their actions, but on His love. John Bunyan continues the water theme and encourages the doubting Christian to rest in God's flowing grace.

Does this water of life run like a river, like a broad, full, and deep river? Then let no man, be his transgressions ever so many, fear at all because there is enough to save his soul and more to spare.

Nothing has been more common to many, than to doubt the grace of God: a thing most unbecoming a sinner of anything in the world. To break the law is a fact foul enough; but to question the sufficiency of the grace of God to save is worse than sin.

Therefore, despairing soul, for it is to you I speak, hold

back your mistrust, cast off your mindless fears, hang your misgivings upon the hedge, and believe. You have a sufficient invitation to believe: a river is before your face.

And as for your lack of goodness and good works, let that by no means daunt you. This is a river of life-giving water, with streams of grace and mercy. There is, as I said, enough within to help you, for grace brings all that is wanting to the soul. You, therefore, have nothing to do—I mean as to the curing of your soul of its doubts and fears and despairing thoughts—but to drink and live forever.

-JOHN BUNYAN

> *Can you doubt, if God is love,*
> *If to all His mercies move?*
> *Will you not His Word receive?*
> *Will you not His oath believe?*
> -JOHN WESLEY

God's Purpose for His People—Preach the Good News

[Jesus said,] "Go into all the world and preach the good news to all creation."

MARK 16:15 NIV

When Christ told us disciples to go out into the world and to preach the Gospel, we were to follow His example. He didn't hold giant rallies or revival meetings. Instead, Christ met in homes and taught with simple examples from everyday life. Joanna P. Moore, a white missionary who worked with newly freed African-American slaves in the late 1800s, writes about the importance of being a present help to those with whom we seek to share the Gospel.

There is no place too lowly or dark for our feet to enter and no place so high and bright that it doesn't need the touch of the light that we carry from the cross. There is no man, woman, or child that is so far sunken in sin that our hands cannot reach them—while God holds us up.

We are the highway and hedge workers, who are also able to expound the Scriptures. We can help a tired mother cut out clothes for her child, and meanwhile teach both mother and child the Gospel. We not only pray for the sick, but we also cook them a tempting bite to eat. We are equally at home in the parlor or the kitchen.... We live among the people, and mingle freely with them, so that we may be a present help in time of trouble.

We have never learned how to stand on a pedestal and hand out the Gospel at the end of a forty-foot pole, because we remember that those who have helped us the most are the persons who came up close to us and clasped our hands, kindly smoothed the pain from our aching heads, and sat down beside us, and whispered words of love and hope. Oh, yes, they lived their beautiful lives where we could see and feel their uplifting power. Therefore we have concluded that we will comfort others with the comfort with which we ourselves were comforted. (See 2 Corinthians 1:3-5.) This is the kind of Christian workers that the people of all races need this very day.

-JOANNA P. MOORE

As we are comforting others, we will feel comfort flowing from God. When we help and encourage others, we end up being encouraged ourselves as well.

> *In the highways in the hedges*
> *I'll be somewhere a workin' for my Lord.*
> -MAYBELLE CARTER

Go in Peace

*"Go in peace, and may the God of Israel grant you
what you have asked of him."*
1 SAMUEL 1-17 NIV

When Jesus healed, often the next thing He said was, "Go in peace." He told the woman in Mark 5:34 NIV, "Your faith has healed you. Go in peace and be freed from your suffering."

When we encounter Christ, His presence heals us. He heals our emotional suffering, our worries, our troubles, our memories, and our physical health. But as He heals, He will always tell us to "Go in peace." His peace is truly beyond our understanding. It will outlast all of our problems. When we go on and live in His peace and love, we are able to be well in the face of the next troubling circumstance.

Christ desires our peace and our joy. His peace and love cover a multitude of problems and pains. When we ask for help and healing, He will always bless us and give us peace.

Ask now for His mercy and grace to overflow in your life, and then "go in peace."

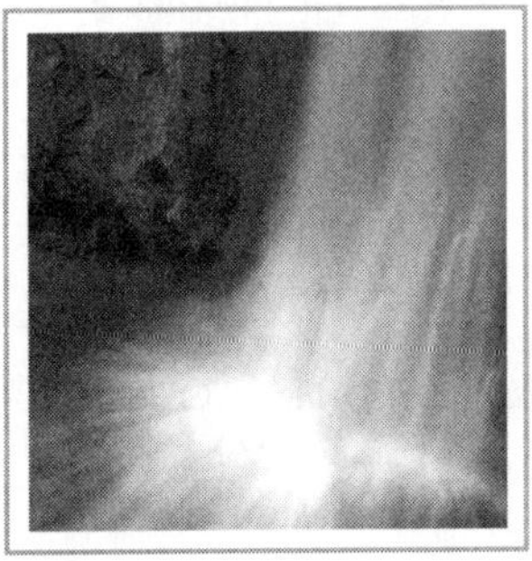

Additional copies of this and other
Honor Books products are available from your local bookseller.

Other titles in this series:

Water from the Rock: Classic Edition
Water from the Rock: African-American Edition
Water from the Rock: Meditations on Grace and Hope

If you have enjoyed this book, or if it has had an impact on your life,
we would like to hear from you.

Please contact us at:

Honor Books, Dept. 201
4050 Lee Vance View
Colorado Springs, CO 80918
Or visit our Web site:
www.cookministries.com

HONOR HB BOOKS

Inspiration and Motivation for the Seasons of Life